EVIDENCE on QUALITY SCHOOLING

Education Now 1

Education Now Series No. 1.
EVIDENCE on QUALITY SCHOOLING

Published in 2022 by Connor Court Publishing Pty Ltd

Copyright © Scott Prasser, David Robertson and Helen Tracey

All rights reserved. No part of this book may be reproduced or transmitted in any form or by any means, electronic or mechanical, including photo copying, recording or by any information storage and retrieval system, without prior permission in writing from the publisher.

Connor Court Publishing Pty Ltd
PO Box 7257
Redland Bay QLD 4165
sales@connorcourt.com
www.connorcourt.com
Phone 0497-900-685

Printed in Australia

ISBN: 9781922815002

Cover Design Ian James.

Evidence on Quality Schooling

Scott Prasser, David Robertson and Helen Tracey

Connor Court Publishing

Contents

Abbreviations	7
Preface	9
Series Editors	10
Acknowledgements	10
Introduction	11
Part 1 Interpreting the Evidence	**15**
The private and public benefits of a good education	15
Measuring skills – where to look for objective data	16
Early childhood education	22
Measuring quality – a more complex issue	24
Making sense of the evidence – a complex web	**33**
Family background	34
Individual differences	37
Assessing the research	40
Part 2 What makes a difference in schools	**43**
Funding	43
Class size	46
School size	48
Teacher attributes	49
Teacher practice – the curriculum, and how it's delivered	55
Assessment	61
Technology	63
Behaviour	64
School ethos	65
Well-being	66
High expectations	69
Academic streaming	69
Single sex schools	71
Extra-curricular activities	71

Parents, and homework	73
The physical environment	74
School leadership	75
Part 3 What the latest performance data show	**77**
International data	**77**
PISA	78
TIMSS	83
PIRLS	86
Australian data – readiness for school	**88**
Australian data – NAPLAN	**91**
In a word... some conclusions	**97**
References	100

Abbreviations

ACARA	Australian Curriculum, Assessment and Reporting Authority
AEDC	Australian Early Development Census
ACER	Australian Council for Educational Research
ATAR	Australian Tertiary Admission Rank
EU	European Union
GDP	Gross Domestic Product
IAEEA	International Association for the Evaluation of Educational Achievement
IQ	Intelligence Quotient
LBOTE	Language Background Other Than English
LSAC	Longitudinal Study of Australian Children
LSAY	Longitudinal Survey of Australian Youth
NAPLAN	National Assessment Program – Literacy and Numeracy
OECD	Organisation for Economic Co-operation and Development
PIRLS	Progress in International Reading Literacy Study
PISA	Program for International Student Assessment
STEM	Science, technology, engineering and maths
TIMMS	Trends in International Mathematics and Science Study

Preface

The *Education Now* series was developed to present information about modern-day schooling that is grounded in research and evidence. The papers in the series take as their starting point the conviction that quality schooling serves the best interests of a nation, since an educated citizenry is the foundation of a vibrant and productive society, and is in the best interests also of each individual, as a high quality schooling experience sets the scene for a productive, fulfilling and healthy life.

Up to date, relevant and objective evidence is hard to access for parents seeking to make the best decisions about their children's education. Much of the information readily available is contradictory and confusing, because education is a complex process, dependent on many players – different levels of government, school authorities, school staff, families and individual students – and shaped by contextual factors such as location and culture. Discussion in the media about schooling can often be polemical, partisan and sensationalised, while academic studies can be difficult to penetrate and often do not have general application.

The *Education Now* series aims to synthesise the wealth of information that is available on the important features of schooling and present this in an accessible and objective way. Each book in the series draws on sound data and reputable research findings and makes this evidence accessible to general readers keen to understand the wide range of influences on each student's experience of school and to recognise what actions, by governments, schools and families, will make a difference.

The Series covers:
- what works best to give students a high quality schooling experience
- how schools are funded including history, recent developments, and the impact of funding on education performance
- the importance of the school curriculum and how it is taught
- trends in the performance of Australian students
- the shared responsibility for the outcomes of schooling, among governments, schools, families and students

Series Editors

Dr Scott Prasser has worked in federal and state governments in senior public service research and policy roles and held several academic positions. He has served as senior adviser to federal ministers across education, immigration, and regional health. He holds undergraduate and postgraduate qualifications from Queensland and Griffith universities.

David Robertson has worked in the education sector in Victoria and Queensland for several decades. A qualified economist, his expertise covers school funding, Commonwealth and state education legislation and regulation and government policy processes. He has served on school education committees and working groups at ministerial, departmental, and stakeholder levels.

Helen Tracey has worked in research roles in universities following a career in public policy, mainly education policy, with the Commonwealth government. Helen has academic qualifications in political science, public policy and education from the Australian National University and the University of London (Institute of Education) and has completed numerous research projects on education and related areas.

Acknowledgements

The Editors acknowledge advice on each of the reports by a number of teachers, current and former principals from both the public and non-government sectors and leading education experts like Professor John Hattie of the University of Melbourne.

Evidence on quality schooling

Introduction

The belief that a good education is what equips people for a better life, contemporary as it sounds, can be dated back to the Greek philosopher Aristotle in the fourth century BC.

The classical conception of education attributed to Aristotle, as all round, balanced development, a combination of reason and practice in play, music, physical exercise, debate and the study of science and philosophy, has resonance today in the broad-ranging functions of modern schooling. This view of education as central to personal fulfilment has been echoed through the ages, with the added understanding that a good education not only benefits the individual but also society and the state. While Aristotle relied on logic and insight for his beliefs, modern day political leaders can draw on a convincing base of scientific evidence to show that an educated population is the foundation for building a vibrant and productive nation, a strong economy and a good society.

Heads of state the world over have been informed by this evidence in putting education at the centre of their national policy-making. From South Africa, Nelson Mandela saw education as "the most powerful weapon which you can use to change the world", its power extending "beyond the development of skills we need for economic success. It can contribute to nation-building and reconciliation." In the United Kingdom, before becoming Prime Minister in 1997 Tony Blair famously foreshadowed that his government's top three priorities would be "education, education, education", recognising this as the best economic policy there is. He described a good school as one where children gain the basic tools for life and work, but also learn the joy of life – the exhilaration of music, the excitement of sport, the beauty of art, the magic of science – and the value of life – what it is to be responsible citizens who give something back to their community.

In the United States, President Obama stated that in the 21st century, the best anti-poverty program is a world-class education. Michelle Obama often emphasised her belief in the importance of education, especially for girls and for children from poorer families: "The ability to read, write and analyze; the confidence to stand up and demand justice and equality; the qualifications and connections to get your foot in that door and take your seat at that table – all of that starts with education."

In Australia, while federation gave the education power to the states, in the 1950s and 1960s Prime Minister Robert Menzies (1949-66) gradually extended the Commonwealth Government's involvement in schooling, driven by the conviction that "Our great function when we approach the problem of education is to equalise opportunity to see that every boy and girl has a chance to develop whatever faculties he or she may have, because this will be a tremendous contribution to the good life for the nation". The Menzies Government introduced national funding programs for students and school facilities which laid the foundation for a gradually increasing role for the Commonwealth to pursue measures to serve the national interest in having a well-educated population although the states' constitutional power over school education limits the scope of Commonwealth intervention. As Prime Minister, Julia Gillard gave credit to Menzies for understanding "the power of education as a force for good, a force for equity and a force for change".

The other 20th century Australian Prime Minister recognised as a champion of education quality and opportunity was Gough Whitlam (1972-75) who based his education policy agenda on the belief that "We are all diminished when any of us are denied proper education. The nation is the poorer – a poorer economy, a poorer civilisation, because of this human and national waste."

The evidence that supports these grand claims for the value of a high quality education and a highly educated population is overwhelming. Demographic data confirm that across the population and over a lifetime, better education outcomes are linked to better health, greater employment stability and job satisfaction, stronger earnings capacity and improved citizenship. Economic analysis shows that an educated citizenry is the foundation for building a vibrant and productive nation. Many Australians as individuals have seen for themselves how a good education can be a pathway to a productive, fulfilling and healthy life. After family, a person's experience of schooling and further education has the strongest influence on their life outcomes. Any policy stance promoting the objective of higher quality schooling will therefore remain uncontested.

What does remain contested however is the means to this end: how to determine the right approach, in policy and practice, to achieve all the high and worthy expectations we have of the education system. While the public in general and parents in particular have an abiding interest in Australian schooling, views about what works best to give students a high quality schooling experience are many and varied, and often contradictory and confusing. Fads and fashions in teaching and in school management and design abound. The practices involved in teaching and in managing schools are highly politicised, with the labels 'conservative' and 'progressive' readily, meaninglessly and harmfully attached to particular approaches.

This book sets out to take party politics and ideology out of the analysis of good schooling. It examines research and practical evidence about what works best in schools and sets out to present this in a way that enables those interested to make their own informed judgements when reacting to new education policy measures or assessing the programs and practices in the schools with which they are associated.

It starts in **Part 1** by re-asserting the importance of high quality schooling and pointing out where to look for reliable data. **Part 2** highlights the critical success factors for quality schooling, which come down to skilled and talented teaching, a sound and demanding curriculum, high expectations of all students, and a positive and supportive school climate. **Part 3** reports in general terms on the various data sets that measure the 'success' of Australian education, a report card that confirms our good fortune as a nation in having a high quality, reasonably equitable schooling system but one where there is room for improvement if all students are to have their best chance of a good life and if Australia is to remain economically competitive in our region and internationally.

Part 1
Interpreting the evidence

The private and public benefits of a good education

Evidence on the value to individuals and nations of good schooling has built up over recent decades and shows incontrovertibly why we should all be attentive to school quality. It is in our self-interest as well as the national interest to support the best schooling system and the best local schools we can possibly have. A large body of evidence, based on reams of data and sophisticated statistical analysis conducted over time and in many different settings, shows the extent to which individuals and nations reap the benefits of a high quality schooling system.

That such a finding accords with the lived experience of so many of us helps its ready acceptance. We can recognise the private returns to an individual over a lifetime from a good education in ourselves and others. People with a good education will almost always earn substantially higher incomes, experience greater employment stability and job satisfaction, enjoy better health for themselves and their families, and be more engaged citizens. The benefits are much more than the monetary ones that can be readily measured; they are associated with quality of life and they accrue over a lifetime.

> *It is in our self-interest as well as the national interest to support the best schooling system and the best local schools we can possibly have.*

The importance of being well educated has increased over time. Economists estimate that as economies develop and require higher levels of skill, a quality education becomes even more important in determining a person's labour market outcomes. While people with lower education qualifications may still find employment opportunities, their prospects are much more precarious as technologies advance.

Investment in education is a costly business for governments, but the decision to prioritise education spending is based on clear expectations about the future benefits this will bring to the nation, economically and socially. This is a perfect example of evidence-based policy, almost universally adopted by democracies the world over and embedded also in international development goals. Whether that education is provided publicly or privately, governments are concerned with education as a public good, in the sense that the country as a whole is better off the more there is of it, and the higher its quality.

The converse is equally true. International studies show plainly that countries with lower education participation and poorer school outcomes are also behind in economic and social indicators. Decades of economic evidence confirm the connection between a well-educated population and national productivity and social cohesion, stability and engagement. Equally, many economic and social problems, from crime rates to welfare dependence, are linked to low levels of skill and ability and a poor school experience. More recent analysis reveals the strong causal relationship between education achievement and economic and social indicators – it is more than a statistical correlation; a high level of skills and knowledge in the population is the reason for higher productivity and economic growth.

Measuring skills – where to look for objective data

Data on the impact of quality education are available from a range of sources. Perhaps the most reliable and respected source of international comparative data on education investment and performance relevant to Australia is the OECD, which has been engaged for over sixty years in collecting and analysing evidence on social and economic issues. Other dependable sources are studies conducted under the auspices of intergovernmental bodies such as the World Bank and European Union, and the work of scholarly economic analysts such as Eric Hanushek and Ludger Woessmann who specialise in scrutinising educational outcome data for its meaning and significance, establishing associations, co-relationships and causal connections and attempting to measure them. The 2021 Nobel Prize in economics was awarded to three academic economists, David Card, Joshua Angrist and Guido Imbens, for their work using natural experiments showing, among other results, the causal role quality schooling has on earnings and stability of employment.

Comparable analysis of the relationship between aspects of schooling and education and economic outcomes in Australia is undertaken by the Productivity Commission, whose mandate is to provide independent, quality research to the Australian Government on economic, social and environmental issues affecting the welfare of Australians. The Australian Bureau of Statistics is also a valuable repository for hard data on education. Responsibility for analysis of the data however is dispersed among government authorities, research bodies, think tanks and individual academics, not all of whom approach the task disinterestedly.

> *Research consistently identifies the importance of education to GDP growth and productivity.*

Econometric modelling by and for the OECD continues to confirm and measure the very large impact on national economies of improvements in education participation and achievement. Research consistently identifies the importance of education to GDP growth and productivity. Across the OECD, the impact on the economy of one additional year of education is quantified as between 3% and 6% growth in the level of output per capita. About half the economic growth in OECD countries over the past 50 years has been attributed to higher education attainment, and particularly the higher education attainment of half the population, women.

The impact of education attainment on employment rates and earnings is also significant. On average across OECD countries in 2016, the employment rate for adults (25-64 year-olds) without upper secondary education was 59%, while for those with upper secondary or post-secondary non-tertiary education as their highest attainment it was 77%, and for tertiary-educated adults, 86%. The same study shows employment rates for Australia as 62% for adults without upper secondary education, compared with 79% for those with upper secondary or post-secondary non-tertiary education, and 85% for those with tertiary education. In general, both employment rates and earnings increase with additional time spent in education post-school.

Unemployment rates are especially high among young adults lacking upper secondary education – almost twice as high as for those with upper or post-secondary attainment. The expectation that emerges from studies undertaken recently, in the shadow of the COVID-19 pandemic, is that those with lower educational attainment will be even more vulnerable following the health crisis of 2020 and 2021.

Both employment prospects and employment stability are at stake. Higher levels of education attainment reduce the likelihood that a worker will work only part-time or part of a year. Greater educational attainment also brings increasing rewards. On average across OECD countries, full-time workers with upper secondary or post-secondary non-tertiary education earn 25% more than those without, while those with a tertiary degree earn 54% more than those with an upper secondary education.

More fine-grained analysis of the link between education and economic outcomes, for individuals and for countries, shows clearly that even more important than quantitative measures of education attainment are indicators of the quality of education provision. Until relatively recently, education quality was primarily measured in terms of participation and years of schooling completed. Only fifty or so years ago, a major policy objective of governments was to increase school retention and avoid high dropout rates, in the expectation that keeping young people in school would lead to greater employment prospects and stability for individuals and economic growth for nations. Hence laws in most countries providing for compulsory schooling and increasing minimum school leaving ages which have had national economic and intergenerational social effects. That ground has shifted. We now have the capability of measuring quality as well as quantity, and can show that it is knowledge rather than just time in school that has the greater impact on an individual's life chances and national economic growth.

Empirical evidence shows convincingly that improvements in the quality of learning outcomes, over and above time spent in schooling and funding levels, are associated with a stronger economic impact, especially once a threshold level of education participation is exceeded. The higher the quality of education, the more productive the nation. After examining the many determinants of economic growth, researchers have found that differences in cognitive skill levels, as shown by better results in national and international testing regimes, explain the majority of differences in economic growth rates across OECD and European countries, while education performance deficits explain serious shortfalls in economic performance relative to economic possibilities. Higher cognitive skills are systematically related to higher wages, greater employment stability and faster economic growth.

Not all skills are equal however. The basic skills of literacy and numeracy are paramount, as a foundation for further learning. In their exploration of the link between skills, higher labour productivity and GDP per capita, Hanushek and Woessmann (2020) examined the impact of problem-solving skills as well as literacy and numeracy and found that numeracy achievement proved to be the key to growth. On average, a one standard deviation increase in numeracy skills was associated with an 18% wage increase across prime-age workers. The proportion of high and low achievers in numeracy in a country is also significant. A larger share of low achievers is associated with lower economic growth, and a higher proportion of high achievers is associated with greater economic prosperity.

> The basic skills of literacy and numeracy are paramount, as a foundation for further learning.

This particular study by Hanushek and Woessman makes the point that for a nation, a higher level of educational achievement by itself may contribute to, but will not guarantee, growth. Education quality is a necessary though not sufficient condition for prosperity. In countries with the highest economic growth, educational quality is reinforced by a sound framework of economic institutions, such as an openness to international trade and security of property rights. The benefits of higher skill levels are better realised in open economies.

The international student testing results most commonly used as a measure of a nation's skill level, for making education comparisons between countries, and as a base for econometric modelling of the impact of education achievement come from the **PISA** (Program for International Student Assessment) survey, conducted every three years under the auspices of the OECD to test how well young people, at the age of 15, are prepared for life and work beyond school. The PISA tests, administered since 2000, and now with about 80 countries participating, are recognised primarily as a rich source of sound data on schooling that countries can delve into to explore for relevance to their own social and education settings. The tests are not an accountability mechanism but serve as a yardstick for measuring and comparing performance.

The tests are a long way from the standardised basic skills tests that are much maligned in education research and public discussion. They do measure basic knowledge, but they are also designed to assess how well 15-year-olds can solve problems and apply their knowledge and skills to real world situations in the three domains of science, maths and reading literacy. At the same time they collect a great deal of contextual information about participating students, their schools, teachers and families which throws light on the many overlapping factors involved in education success in a particular context and generates insights into those elements of schooling and society most often associated with high and low performance.

PISA results are reported on a set of scales that enable comparisons to be made between average scores – both an overall average, and an average score in each of the three domains tested – as well as between the proportions of students at different levels of proficiency. The share of high and low performers is an important factor in measuring a country's PISA success.

At the national level, improvements in skill levels as measured by increases in PISA scores are closely related to higher economic growth. Recent studies for the European Union (EU) by Hanushek and Woessman (2020) have quantified the enormous potential economic benefits that would occur in EU countries over time from reducing the share of low achievers in PISA, and from increasing student achievement by 25 PISA points. The largest gains, measured as a 7.3% increase in discounted future GDP, come from increasing average performance. The impact of reducing the share of low achievers to no more than 15% produces a 3.9% increase. An Australian study undertaken in 2016 by Deloitte Access Economics estimates that an increase of 4.4 points in Australia's average PISA score in maths would increase GDP by 0.14% once the effect was fully realised in the labour force, equivalent to a gain of A$2 billion.

In a few countries where analysis based on individual students' PISA results and longitudinal data has been undertaken, high PISA scores are associated with higher post-school education, skilled employment and higher earnings for individuals.

Early childhood education

While the evidence showing the benefits of a quality school education is strong and persuasive, even more convincing is the case made for the value of effective early childhood education. Advances in our understanding of economics and a revolution in neuroscience leading to better knowledge of how the brain develops have established that for governments, the greatest economic and social returns come from investment in early childhood development. Findings generated from cross-disciplinary studies into the social determinants of health, inspired and led since the late 1980s by the Canadian scholar Dr Fraser Mustard, have shown that interventions in the early years enable children to be successful earlier and save significant public resources later. Poor early childhood experiences are associated with learning difficulties in school. If these can be addressed early, the results are pronounced, manifested in higher achievement through the school years, and better health and well-being in adult life.

Neuroscience has shown how the early years of development establish the basic architecture and function of the brain. In the first few years of a child's life, the brain develops rapidly to build the foundation of cognitive and character skills such as attentiveness, motivation, self-control and sociability necessary for success in school, health, career and life. Academic performance at school, and the health status of adults have been shown to have their antecedents in early childhood. Nurture in the early years has major effects throughout the life cycle. It is the foundation for future learning. Children arrive in the school system with many pre-determined capacities for learning, as well as behaviour and health attributes which are predicated on their early experiences. Teachers have to build on the quality of a child's early childhood experiences.

The economic and social returns on investment in early learning can be observed in improved educational achievement, better health and well-being in adult life, higher economic returns for individuals, and financial benefits for governments. The saving to governments for every $1 invested in the early childhood years has been measured as a reduction in later education spending by as much as $3 in school age children and $8 on adult education. Measurable public returns are generated through increased earnings, improved health outcomes, and reduced social costs. School based programs are less effective in enhancing the language and maths skills of children who have had poor early child development. Countries that have quality universal early development programs for families with young children have been found to outperform countries in which early development programs are chaotic or where social supports for needy families are lacking, and participation in quality early learning activities is associated with better performance in international testing.

> The economic and social returns on investment in early learning can be observed in improved educational achievement, better health and well-being in adult life, higher economic returns for individuals, and financial benefits for governments.

The key though is the quality of the early learning provision. Poorly designed or delivered programs do not bring the same returns, educationally, socially or economically. The beneficial effects of even high quality early childhood interventions have been found to fade out in later years in terms of cognitive gains, even though the benefits of the programs in developing non-cognitive skills such as optimism and resilience endure, leading to a greater likelihood of participants graduating from high school and being in employment. The international testing regimes which cover Grade 4 students (TIMSS and PIRLS, see below) establish a positive relationship between pre-school educational activities, either formal pre-primary education, or frequent engagement at home with parents in literacy and numeracy activities, and achievement in maths, science and reading.

Nobel prize-winning American economist James Heckman has measured the economically significant returns to the community of high quality early childhood programs for children who do not have a home environment that encourages early learning. Every dollar spent delivers a 13% per annum return on investment, through better outcomes in education, health, social behaviours, and employment, reducing taxpayer costs and with beneficial effects on a nation's productivity.

This is the evidence that underpins public policies in Australia supporting disadvantaged families, and the provision of quality child care and early learning. It is the rationale for the administration of the Australian Early Development Census (AEDC), a nationwide census that has been conducted every three years since 2009 to show how well young Australian children have developed as they start their first year of full-time education.

Measuring quality – a more complex issue

While objective, numerical measures have been established to indicate the return to individuals and nations from educational attainment and achievement, it is a more difficult exercise to specify a measure of school quality. School quality is a complex and amorphous concept, not lending itself easily to quantification. Attempts at measuring quality are confounded by the many and varied goals of schooling, and the many variables that affect education outcomes, both those associated with the particular school as well as those associated with each student.

Schools have a broad set of goals, as can be seen in the variety of aspirational values and objectives expressed through such things as the school mottos displayed prominently in school grounds. These mottos create a first impression of a school and what it regards as most important in the education it will provide its community.

The goals of schooling generally encompass learning outcomes alongside a range of non-academic objectives which have economic, cultural, social and personal dimensions. Economically, education is expected to enable students to become financially responsible and independent. This is captured by school mottos such as *"Learning for life"*, *"A foundation for the future"* and *"Opening doors through literacy"*. Culturally, education aims to enable students to understand and appreciate their own cultures and respect the diversity of others, as emphasised in mottos such as *"Advancing human understanding"* and *"Making lives better"*. Socially, education should enable young people to become active, responsible and compassionate citizens, with this sense of social responsibility and service to others reflected in such slogans as *"Work hard and be kind"*, *"Learn well today, live well tomorrow"* and *"Making the World a Better Place with More Education, Knowledge and Wisdom"*. Personally, education is expected to enable young people to engage healthily with the world within them as well as the world around them; hence common school mottos such as *"Know Thyself"* and *"Truth and Courage"*.

Few schools manage to capture the full range of their goals for students in a pithy motto, but it is obvious even from these few examples that many of the goals set will never be measured by objective data. Proxy measures, relying heavily on achievement outcomes, have to be used, and judgements made. While academic achievement as measured by student performance in national and international testing regimes and, for secondary students, in end-of-school results, is a strong indicator of school quality, it does not tell the whole story. It does not measure kindness or social responsibility, wisdom or courage. Academic learning is central to schooling, but it is not everything.

Student performance data from tests are however an indispensable backdrop for any informed commentary on school quality. They enable comparisons to be made and trends over time to be studied but they are most useful when they are contextualised, as they are for example in analysis of the previously mentioned PISA survey where associations and relationships are established between test results and various characteristics of the student, family, school and education system. The OECD produces several hefty volumes of material for each PISA cycle, reporting on the international results and contextual data in forensic detail for countries, students and schools. Individual countries gain understanding and knowledge by scrutinising their own results in the same depth, interpreting the results in the context of their own education systems and learning from them.

This deep analysis generates valuable cross-country information and enables each participating country to review its own performance against a range of objective benchmarks. PISA has been conducted in Australia every three years since 2000, most recently in 2018, testing the cognitive skills of 15 year olds in science, mathematics and literacy. It is conducted as a sample study, with a representative group of over 14,000 students in over 700 schools participating in 2018. Each PISA cycle emphasises a particular skill area. In 2018, the focus was on reading. PISA 2018 also included two optional assessment domains, 'global competence', in which Australia did not participate, and 'financial literacy' which was administered here. The testing due in 2021 has been postponed to 2022, because of the impact on schooling of the coronavirus pandemic.

Other international measures which also inform research and analysis of education achievement and trends are **TIMSS** (Trends in International Mathematics and Science Study, last administered in 2019) and **PIRLS** (Progress in International Reading Literacy, conducted in 2016 and again in 2021). Both these tests are directed by the International Association for the Evaluation of Educational Achievement (IAEEA). TIMSS is an assessment of the maths and science knowledge and understanding of students in grades 4 and 8 and is conducted every 4 years. It is a more curriculum focused international test than PISA. PIRLS tests the reading achievement of 4th graders every 5 years. The Australian sample involved in TIMSS is nearly 600 schools and almost 15,000 students, while for PIRLS it is over 300 schools and more than 6,000 students.

The comprehensive analysis of the outcomes of PISA, TIMSS and PIRLS results has provided a rich bank of data on the connection between elements of schooling and both performance and equity. The results have had a significant influence on education policymaking worldwide. Their value goes well beyond the comparative test scores and rankings they produce. A substantial research effort has gone into identifying the success factors of those countries with impressive or significantly improved results and exploring their relevance elsewhere.

> The comprehensive analysis of the outcomes of PISA, TIMSS and PIRLS results has provided a rich bank of data on the connection between elements of schooling and both performance and equity.

International testing results always need to be interpreted in the light of the many different social, cultural and educational differences influencing the outcomes. While informative, they are no basis for fully understanding national education performance. The results highlight factors related to achievement which then can be tested against domestic data and knowledge. The national equivalent measure of school achievement in Australia, providing a database for measuring the performance of schools over time and for making comparisons between schools, jurisdictions, geographic areas and social groups is **NAPLAN** (National Assessment Program – Literacy and Numeracy). The NAPLAN tests are standardised basic skills tests administered annually since 2008 to the full population of students in grades 3, 5, 7 and 9 in schools across the country (with some allowable exemptions). Results from the NAPLAN tests are published at school and state level, and are made available online on the *My School* website. Individual student reports are also prepared, for use by teachers and parents.

NAPLAN results provide a bank of information at the school, system, state and national level for accountability purposes. They provide governments and school authorities with an objective and sound evidence base for assessing student achievement in basic literacy and numeracy against national standards and for comparing various cohorts of students. Analysis of test results at this level can reveal areas of need, examples of success, and changes over time. Schools themselves can use this independently collected data to examine their own teaching strengths and weaknesses and to monitor student progress.

The value of the test results as a measure of school quality however is limited by their focus on basic skills and minimum standards. The rationale for testing the foundational skills of literacy and numeracy is that they are the basis for learning in all curriculum areas. While they are not in themselves sufficient for individuals to succeed in life, the achievement of minimum standards in the basic skills is a necessary component of quality, but only an indication rather than a measure of a school's overall quality. NAPLAN results represent but one point of data within an array of other assessments and information. Like PISA, they can be used to establish relationships and associations between performance and particular aspects of schooling and student background, to inform education policymakers.

NAPLAN has its fair share of critics, echoing familiar charges laid against standardised testing around the world. Problems with standardised testing programs in other countries have been extensively canvassed in the research literature, especially where high stakes are attached to the test results, for instance if they are used to penalise or reward teachers, stigmatise schools or lead to grade repetition for students. Overreliance on tests, it has been observed, will have perverse effects on classroom teaching, distorting teaching practice and narrowing the curriculum, privileging literacy and numeracy over other areas of learning, over-emphasising minimum competencies at the expense of creative and analytical skills and devaluing high academic achievement. At their worst, high stakes tests can create passive learning environments and stultify teacher creativity. Critics of NAPLAN regularly rehearse these generic charges and also claim the tests induce anxiety and stress in students.

In any objective sense, NAPLAN cannot be described as a high stakes test – no jobs are lost, no funding sacrificed, there are no academic repercussions for students. How a school incorporates the NAPLAN testing regime into its overall program can be seen as a signal of its commitment to the broad goals of a quality education. Some schools and school communities do over-emphasise the importance of NAPLAN, inflating its significance and thus encouraging teaching to the test and over-preparation at the expense of a broader, more engaging teaching program, and generating test anxiety. The validity of concerns about the stress NAPLAN testing imposes on students is contingent on the school's approach to NAPLAN – when students are familiar with the format of the tests and teachers accurately convey its value and application, there is no reason for anxiety. It is also argued that the experience of two-yearly NAPLAN testing will increase students' familiarity with external testing and thus reduce the anxiety that accompanies genuinely high-stakes tests they encounter in other contexts. Assessment is after all an essential part of schooling, with the aim of benefiting students.

A regime of national literacy and numeracy testing was introduced in Australia in the 1990s because of the absence of a national evidence base against which to test claims about high or low performance. Oft-expressed concerns about falling standards could not be validated with available data in our federal political system where each state had its own approach to testing. 'Concerns' are not always a reflection of reality. NAPLAN was designed to provide the data necessary to assess performance levels and trends on a consistent national basis, building on the foundation of a long history of literacy and numeracy testing at state level. By 2008, students in each state were sitting the same tests. The designers of NAPLAN were aware that basic skills testing with a focus on achieving measured minimum targets would provide only an incomplete measure of school quality and could provide a false impression of quality if these minimum standards were set too low, one of many criticisms of NAPLAN. Efforts to achieve measured targets for school performance can result in effort substitution, teaching to the test instead of covering the broad curriculum, thus hitting the target – reaching the minimum standard – but missing the point – a quality schooling experience.

In addition to their value in providing independently collected visible information on achievement levels, the NAPLAN tests are designed to benefit students and aid teachers by identifying strengths and weaknesses which classroom teachers can then address. The usefulness of NAPLAN as a diagnostic tool however is predicated on the results being known to teachers early enough in the school year for them to take action, and teachers using them appropriately. The tests have been held in May each year, but will in future be held earlier in the school year which, together with the online administration of the tests, will enable faster, earlier provision of data to the classroom teacher.

Labelling NAPLAN as a high-stakes test and denigrating it, as some interest groups and governments do, can be interpreted as a shirking of accountability, a wish to keep poor performance hidden from the public eye and a refusal to address problems. Ostensibly, the rationale given by those arguing for the abandonment of NAPLAN or suggesting that the results be kept from the public is that poor results will stigmatise poorly performing schools and poorly achieving students. The further argument is made that other evidence such as parent and teacher views outweigh the evidence that comes from data. However, refusing to acknowledge that there is a proportion of students struggling to meet basic literacy and numeracy standards, for whatever reasons, will only aggravate the problem and stand in the way of finding solutions.

Another familiar indicator of academic achievement for secondary school students is their end-of-school results, particularly the university entry scores of Year 12 students. These go by different names in different states but are now reported on a common scale, a number between zero and 99.95, as the Australian Tertiary Admission Rank (**ATAR**), based on a student's overall academic performance. Its main purpose is to rank students for university entry. Since academic achievement is an important element of school quality and entry into higher education is a major goal for the majority of senior secondary students, it is valid to draw inferences about the quality of a school on the basis of the success of the Year 12 cohort, taking into account whether or not the school is academically selective and looking at the performance of the group as a whole and comparisons with previous years and similar schools.

Until recently, end of school scores were published widely in the printed media, to celebrate the success of young people and a school. In former days in some states, the results were officially released through the newspapers at the same time as students were advised individually. Publicity now tends to be more localised, with schools choosing to recognise the various achievements of their final year students for the information of their own community, highlighting high ATAR scores but also drawing attention to vocational and non-academic achievements. Research over time has consistently shown the close connection between students' final school results and their later education and employment outcomes, with high academic achievement at school strongly associated with success at university and in professional life. There are of course numerous exceptions that prove that rule, a tribute in part to the many opportunities and paths to post-school study open to young Australians.

Neither NAPLAN results nor ATAR scores are accompanied by the rich set of background and contextual information that is published with the PISA and TIMSS results, but further information about young people's experiences of schooling in Australia and the impact of these on their life chances can be found in longitudinal studies such as the Longitudinal Survey of Australian Youth (**LSAY**) and the Longitudinal Study of Australian Children (**LSAC**). Since the early 1990s, LSAY has followed cohorts of students from high school through to their mid-20s, collecting information about their academic performance at school, participation and achievement in further study, social background, attitudes, workforce participation and income. To date six separate cohorts of more than 10,000 young people each have been studied, illustrating those elements of a young person's social background and school experience that have an impact on their education and employment outcomes later. LSAC was a later development, beginning in 2002 to follow the development of 10,000 children and families across Australia, to study the impact of childhood experiences such as physical health, family circumstances and dynamics and social connections on schooling and life outcomes. These two studies give solid statistical evidence on associations between family and educational experiences in childhood and later education and employment outcomes.

In addition to this wealth of independently collected performance and achievement data, the evidence base on quality schooling includes a plethora of qualitative research and evaluation studies by education researchers, conducted in schools and with teachers. These monitor the impact of particular interventions and aspects of schooling and seek to identify practices and approaches that are expected to lead to higher achievement, either across the board or for particular groups of students.

Making sense of the evidence – a complex web

This wealth of available evidence needs to be interpreted with an understanding of the limitations of the data, an awareness of its source, and consideration of its application in specific contexts. No one set of data is a perfect measure of student achievement or of school quality, but each set provides objective information as a base for exploring the important factors contributing to student success and a quality schooling experience.

Large scale international testing regimes such as PISA for example are robust and informative but they are limited in that they produce 'big data', which does not simply translate into a local setting. International test results are announced for countries in terms of averages, rankings and trends over time, with generalised conclusions. While this provides an essential evidence base for governments responsible for system-wide policy decisions, such a broad-brush approach will not necessarily reflect the everyday experience of schools, classrooms, families and students. Reporting on the data internationally shows distinctions between countries and categories of students, while reporting in Australia shows differences between states and school systems as well, yet the evidence shows that in Australia, as in most countries that perform well in PISA, the greatest variation in achievement is found within schools rather than between them. The aggregation of achievement data to the school level tends to conceal the considerable variation among students within a school, as well as variance in the effectiveness of teachers within schools, by most accounts the most significant school-related factor affecting quality.

> ... the greatest variation in achievement is found within schools rather than between them.

Caution is needed when drawing conclusions about particular schools and students on the basis of population-level data. Institutions and individuals do not perform according to group averages, nor does the average for a population indicate the likelihood for a particular individual. Research findings are never a sufficient basis to draw conclusions about an individual student or a particular school. In the same way, it is not valid to draw generalised conclusions from an individual example, an anecdote or personal experience – especially if that personal experience is dated. We have all been to school, but our recollections and impressions are no substitute for looking at current evidence and examining it in context.

Family background

This caution is particularly relevant in relation to links made between performance data and the socio-economic status of schools and students. Family socio-economic status has long been recognised as being closely linked to schooling outcomes, with the lottery of life – where you are born and who you are born to – considered to be an unfair determining factor in education success. The accident of birth has consequences that can last a lifetime. Students from a socio-economically disadvantaged background are, at a population level, less likely to complete their schooling, and are more likely to repeat a year, have lower scores on tests such as NAPLAN and PISA, and have lower Year 12 attainment.

> While the lottery of birth may be a powerful predictor of education success, evidence shows that family background is far from deterministic...

But at the level of an individual, this trajectory is in no way inevitable. While the lottery of birth may be a powerful predictor of education success, evidence shows that family background is far from deterministic, thanks to the infinite variety in individuals and families, and thanks too to a wide range of health, social and education support programs devised to address elements of disadvantage. While 'big data' consistently show the close correlation between economic disadvantage and education underachievement, the link between the two is not a causal one, nor is it inescapable.

In reporting the results of international and national student achievement tests, the raw scores are generally adjusted with one or two layers of a measurement of socio-economic status, the first layer being a measure of the student's family background, and the second layer an average socio-economic measure for the school. These calculations, which confirm the statistical link between social and economic advantage and better school performance, provide descriptive data showing that at a population level, students from socio-economically disadvantaged family backgrounds and attending schools assessed as relatively less advantaged are less likely to achieve well than their peers from better-off families attending so-called wealthier schools. This establishes an association between socio-economic disadvantage and academic achievement but does not go far towards explaining the reasons for differences in performance. There is a line of argument that the influence of socio-economic status has been overstated and specifically that the second layer of measurement, of a school's socio-economic status, which is applied to both national and international testing data, is no more than a statistical artefact. Emphasising family background as an explanatory factor tends to minimise the significance of poor results by suggesting that expectations should be lower for this cohort of students and also serves to obscure the many individual and school-related factors that directly influence school achievement.

Rich data sources have made it possible to examine more closely the causal connection between socio-economic status and student performance, leading to greater understanding of the aspects of the home environment that have the most influence on students' outcomes. It turns out that it is not wealth or income levels, but the value parents place on education, the environment they provide for learning and how out-of-school time is used that make the difference. The socio-economic measure that is most powerful is the education level of parents.

Sophisticated data analysis suggests that, at the level of the individual as distinct from the group, the significance of socio-economic status on education outcomes may have been greatly overstated. Just as a proportion of students from well-off or well educated families do not do well at school, so many students from less advantaged backgrounds achieve at a high level and enjoy good post-school outcomes. Through analysis of PISA results, it can be seen that between 10% and 20% of variations in student achievement are attributable to a student's socio-economic background, far less than the influence of other factors such as a student's innate ability and the quality of teaching in a school. On average, across the OECD 11% of students are categorised as 'academically resilient', achieving well despite coming from a poor background. For Australia, the figure is just above that, 13%.

There is much interesting research seeking to explain how it is that so many students perform well in school despite a disadvantaged background. Both individual student and school-related characteristics are involved. Analysis of the 2015 and 2018 PISA results, for example, establishes that student motivation, attitudes and belief, and a positive school climate with high expectations of students are critical drivers of achievement, two to three times more powerful than the home environment and just as important as other school and teacher influences.

In part, the significance of family background on performance depends on what measure of 'disadvantage' is used. Family income as a proxy for socio-economic status is only weakly related to student performance. Popular as it may be to attribute a family's influence on their child's education performance to their relative wealth and privilege, the really important factor, far more influential than income, is the education level of parents. Well educated parents tend to value education, have high expectations and encourage achievement, and this variable is associated with students' achievement, motivation and competence. One measure of socio-economic status used in the international testing regimes is an estimate of resources in the home supporting the student, including a measure of the number of books in the home. Living in a home with many books – indicating a home environment that values literacy, the acquisition of knowledge and general academic support – is consistently associated with higher academic achievement.

Individual differences

While too much importance may be assigned to family 'advantage' or 'disadvantage' in explaining differences in achievement, generally too little account is taken of the innate ability of a student. Many robust studies show that it is students themselves and their abilities and predispositions who are the major source of variance in achievement. This is where the lottery of birth is important. Parents pass on to their children their genes as well as a home environment. Intelligence is therefore a key part of the lottery of life, with high intelligence unequally distributed – 50% of intelligence is attributable to genetics, over which an individual has no control – but like social disadvantage, innate intelligence is not deterministic, nor is it static. There is still 50% of intelligence that is not related to genes, influenced by home and school. Brain science shows how intelligence is influenced by nutrition, the home environment and education. Home and environmental influences in childhood affect how and whether genes are expressed, and intelligence develops with learning and motivation.

> While too much importance may be assigned to family 'advantage' or 'disadvantage' in explaining differences in achievement, generally too little account is taken of the innate ability of a student.

Until the 1960s in Australia, a student's ability and potential to do well in school were routinely measured early in primary school through **IQ** (Intelligence Quotient) tests, a ratio of tested mental age to chronological age, usually expressed as a quotient multiplied by 100, where the average score is 100. These tests were gradually abandoned by Australian education systems because of concerns about their legitimacy for truly understanding intellectual capacity and doubts about their appropriateness in a culturally diverse setting. Recognition of the existence and importance of multiple intelligences, including emotional, practical and creative intelligence, also contributed to their abandonment. More tellingly, IQ tests were discredited because of their association with their misguided use in justifying race, class and sex discrimination in some places. The use of intelligence tests is now largely limited to medicine, to help diagnose intellectual disability or assess intellectual potential.

In Australian research into the factors influencing achievement at school, the proxy measure of ability now used is a measure of prior achievement as assessed by NAPLAN, thus relying on a competency and problem-solving test rather than an assessment of intelligence. Analyses of NAPLAN data over time show that a student's prior achievement in NAPLAN tests statistically has a stronger effect on later achievement than family background or any single school-related factor. Achievement builds on past achievement. The Years 3 and 5 NAPLAN results of students are the most significant indicator of their later performance.

This finding is replicated in studies in other countries, based on their own basic skills testing regimes, and in international testing data too. High performance in cognitive skills tests has been shown to have a causal connection to individuals' success in university studies, the stability of their employment and earnings capacity. Longitudinal studies in Australia and elsewhere confirm that achievement at school is a strong and consistent predictor for later education and workforce outcomes.

One well used metric for weighing the relative importance of the various factors that influence student outcomes was developed over ten years ago by John Hattie through a synthesis and analysis of numerous Australian and international research studies. In his much referenced book *Visible Learning* (2009) and subsequent research papers, Hattie acknowledges the importance of factors outside the school, namely the student and the home environment, and assigns over 50% of the responsibility for a student's achievement to outside-school factors, with 50% accounted for by prior achievement and a further 5 to 10% by the student's home environment, including family expectations and encouragement. This leaves the remainder of the differences, 40% to 45%, accounted for by factors within the school. Some reputable studies assign an even higher role in shaping results to innate intelligence and other outside school influences – in some studies, between half and two thirds of the variance in achievement is said to come from students and their families.

The wealth of data harvested from national and international testing results in recent years has only served to shore up the conclusion that while what happens in schools makes a difference, students and their families are not passive agents in the quest for success in school. The absolute measure of their importance may be contested, but intelligence and cognitive ability are critically important to academic achievement and should not be ignored when assessing the factors involved in high and low performance. The reason they often are ignored may be simply that they are not susceptible to influence through policy intervention, but it is important to note that there is a limit to what schools can be expected to achieve. Students' ability and effort are an important part of the total picture.

What the evidence shows is that the individual student, their family and their school experience all contribute in different ways and different degrees to schooling outcomes. Over-reliance on student background factors can lead to the erroneous conclusion that schools and teachers make little difference to student achievement, while giving too much weight to school-related factors ignores the strong influence of individual ability, family circumstance, and personal attributes like study habits and motivation.

Assessing the research

Disentangling the web of interrelated factors involved in a student's schooling experience, including family characteristics, ability, personal attributes and many different aspects of the school itself, is a challenge that has been taken on by numerous expert researchers, asking genuinely open questions, using objective performance data, and applying a variety of statistical techniques to control for different variables. Even then, it remains difficult to unscramble the many influences on performance, to establish causal links and to identify which factors or combination of factors have the most influence on a particular outcome. There are too many confounding, interrelated factors in schooling to allow simple and straightforward answers. Much valuable information has been produced by such studies that then needs to be interpreted in context, to determine if it makes sense in a national or local setting.

Even more caution is needed in interpreting the evidence that comes from qualitative research and evaluation studies of schooling. One challenge in looking at this body of research is to discriminate between those studies that are soundly based and acknowledge alternative positions, and those which are context-specific and advocacy-driven, often using data and information selectively and ignoring any counter-evidence. The evidence base on quality schooling is not completely neutral and objective. It pays to be thoughtful and sceptical in examining it.

There are many reasons why education research findings are contradictory and contested, and why headline-grabbing research findings often do not survive close scrutiny. Studies located in one education context may have little relevance to other schooling systems. Some studies are marred by false assumptions, selective use of data and methodological flaws such as extremely small sample sizes. Some research designs and methods are better than others. Some generalisations based on research will not apply to particular communities, schools and individuals.

The fact that it is possible to find a research study to buttress almost any position on quality schooling points to the importance of using judgement in interpreting findings, being mindful of aspects of the research design such as the context, the openness of the initial research question and the methodology and data sources used and allowing the research to guide and inform rather than determine action.

Sometimes evidence and data are deliberately and mischievously manipulated to suit particular advocacy interests. Survey results in particular can grossly misrepresent reality, notably when a survey is conducted by an interested party and when responses are elicited, often to a set of leading questions, from an unrepresentative or even self-selecting group. Even sets of official data are not immune from misuse to fit a particular narrative. 'Evidence' can be shaped and reported to fit ideological preferences and to underpin special pleading. Such flawed evidence has led from time to time to the introduction of interventions and practices in schools that do nothing to improve academic achievement – indeed, they can have the reverse effect.

In its propensity to ignore objective evidence and take on unproven approaches, the education profession has been compared with medicine as it was over a century ago. Before it became a "mature profession", medicine engaged in such practices as "bleeding, purging, cupping, the administration of infusions of every known plant, solutions of every known metal, most of these based on the weirdest imaginings about the course of disease" (Carnine, 2000, p.9). Following the science has now long characterised the practice of medicine and health policy, as demonstrated recently in responses to the COVID-19 pandemic in those countries where governments relied heavily on expert health advice.

Education too is now in the position of having an extensive and dependable evidence base to draw on. The more familiar the education community is with the nature of that evidence and the interplay of the many factors involved in education achievement, the more scope there is for an informed, questioning approach to proposals for improving the quality of schooling and the more likely it is that those proposals will be soundly based and have their intended effect.

Part 2
What makes a difference in schools

Our knowledge about the features of schooling that are most closely related to student success and well-being has grown immensely over recent years, leaving no excuse for ignoring the evidence when we make demands for changes and improvements in school education. Getting the right mix in the combination of factors that are implicated in students' academic performance and their enjoyment of school involves a little bit of chemistry, and an understanding of how the various components of staff, school, the classroom and the student body affect and interact with each other. Relying on what the hard evidence shows is an essential first step in examining the notion of quality and judging it when you see it. Putting the evidence into context allows us to find explanations for different outcomes of schooling, and press for change where it is needed.

Funding

Despite this sound evidence base, still the most popular public response to any perceived failure of schooling or student achievement – as in most areas of public policy – is to call for additional resources. Public discussion about quality schooling is dominated by questions of funding levels and the distribution of funding, yet the evidence shows this to be a false trail to follow. Such a blinkered focus on resources will often obscure the real issues involved in school quality.

While a positive relationship can be observed between the wealth of a country, as measured by per capita GDP, and its PISA performance, it does not follow that wealthy countries should (or do) invest more and more money in education. A strong positive relationship between funding and international test scores exists for low income nations, but not for high income countries such as Australia. As poorer countries become richer and invest more in education, their PISA results rise; as high income countries get richer and spend more on education, their PISA results remain relatively stable.

Internationally, PISA data over several cycles demonstrate that above a certain level, there is almost no relationship between per student funding and performance. In Australia, increased per student funding over recent years has been accompanied by steadily declining performance, in both international and national tests. This is the case also for many other countries participating in PISA – on average for PISA participating countries, expenditure on schooling has increased by more than 15% over the past decade yet there has been no across-the-board improvement in student learning outcomes.

PISA data over several cycles demonstrate that above a certain level, there is almost no relationship between per student funding and performance.

The evidence from several cycles of PISA shows the positive relationship between investment in education and average performance up to a certain threshold of spending. This threshold level has most recently been calculated as US$50,000 in cumulative expenditure per student from age 6 to 15. Above that level, there is no relationship. Average spending for PISA countries in 2018 was US$89,092, well above the threshold level. Australia, the United Kingdom and the United States all spend more than US$107,000 per student, over twice the threshold amount and 20% more than the average, yet their academic performance is no better (and in some instances worse) than like countries such as Canada, Ireland and New Zealand which spend 10% to 30% less. Nor are the successful Asian country performers in PISA such as Singapore, Hong Kong and Japan particularly high spenders. It is noteworthy that Estonia, which has advanced steadily to the top rankings in PISA and ranked fifth overall in reading in 2018 (and first among OECD countries), spends 30% less than the OECD average. Luxembourg is one of the highest spending countries, spending over four times the threshold amount, but it does not do particularly well in PISA, with a ranking of 37th in reading, outperformed by countries with about one-third its level of spending.

Over many PISA cycles, it has been clear that high spending countries are not necessarily high performing countries, and that countries with similar levels of spending produce very different educational results. Until recently Finland was consistently ranked at the top of the PISA testing cycle and was widely regarded as having the best education system in the world, yet it has never been one of the highest spending countries on schooling. Its success rested on other factors, in particular the high quality of its teaching profession.

Similarly, there is no indication in the data that high spending levels lead to better outcomes for socio-economically disadvantaged students. The highest spending PISA participating countries do not necessarily show better results for low SES students. What the data do show is that variability in the quality of teaching, not the level of funding, is at the heart of performance differences. This is borne out by the evidence that the most significant differences in performance occur not between schools, which may receive different levels of resources, but within schools. The main reason for these differences, outside the individual student and their family background, according to the data, is teacher quality. The link between socio-economic status and performance is weaker in Australia than in other PISA-participating countries, and our data show a greater degree of difference within schools, underlining the need to look at factors other than funding for an explanation of underperformance.

Once the threshold level of expenditure is reached, what matters most is how those resources are distributed, whether they are targeted to elements of schooling where they can make the most difference or dispersed thinly, when the law of diminishing returns applies. The PISA evidence points to the most effective investments being in teacher salaries, teacher professionalism and early childhood education, and in ensuring that the most challenging schools, and the most challenging classes within schools, have effective teachers.

High income countries with high student performance tend to prioritise the quality of teachers over the alternative resource-intensive policy, reducing class size. A case in point is Singapore, whose PISA results over several cycles have been outstanding, following a process of transformation of the education system since 1997. The deliberate on-balance decision taken in the 1990s to prioritise teacher quality rather than teacher numbers as a cornerstone of school improvement has led to greater investment in teacher recruitment, preparation, development and retention and high teacher salaries. As a result, Singapore class sizes are high, in the low 30s, compared with classes in Australia, which are on average in the low 20s.

Class size

In contrast to Singapore's approach, increased investment in Australian schools over the past decade has prioritised general recurrent funding for schools. As a result, average recurrent funding per student has risen from A$11,260 in 2008-09 to A$16,749 in 2018-19 and class size has been reduced, yet this has gone hand in hand with declining performance. This association is a common pattern in international comparisons – at a national or system level, the figures demonstrate unequivocally that smaller average class size is not associated with improved performance. Hence the consistent policy advice emerging from international testing program data that urges governments to invest in better teachers rather than smaller classes.

The evidence at the level of individual schools also produces similar findings. Hundreds of studies have been carried out to assess the impact on groups of students of reducing class size, yet there is very little objective support for this approach. Some studies do show some small effects, depending on the stage of schooling, with smaller classes having been found to have a slight but important and lasting effect on achievement in the early years of schooling, but the major variables are student ability, family background and, above all, teacher expertise.

> *Hence the consistent policy advice emerging from international testing program data that urges governments to invest in better teachers rather than smaller classes.*

Smaller classes are associated with better results mainly to the extent that they reduce discipline problems, raise teacher morale and provide the opportunity for more student-teacher interaction. Unmanaged behavioural problems, especially in the early years, disrupt the teaching of other students and hold back the learning of the whole class. Teachers prefer smaller classes because they see them as more manageable, providing more time for individualised learning and better relations with parents, yet the key to reaping these benefits lies in their own expertise. The positive impact of a smaller class relies on the teacher being able to capitalise on the opportunities for more individualised learning, greater engagement and greater scope for innovation. The evidence shows that many teachers do not adapt their teaching to take advantage of smaller classes.

The conclusion from the evidence is that while a smaller class provides an environment in which teachers can teach differently, this only works to improve performance if teachers have the skills to adapt their approach. PISA data confirm that smaller classes have a measurable effect on student achievement only in countries with a relatively low-quality teaching force, whereas high quality teachers can teach high-quality lessons independent of the size of the class.

School size

Nor does the evidence show any link between school size and student outcomes. Small schools often appeal to parents by offering smaller classes, creating an impression of more personal attention, more opportunities for students to be involved, more cohesion, better discipline and a more caring environment. Certainly there are studies that show the benefits of small schools in terms of achievement that are associated with this sense of community, participation and parent involvement. There are also studies that show lower performance as schools increase in size, despite the advantages associated with large schools such as being able to offer a broader curriculum, more extra-curricular activities and more specialised teaching.

> Nor does the evidence show any link between school size and student outcomes.

The weight of the evidence suggests however that there is no causal link between school size per se and student outcomes. There are other factors at play influencing performance that are more important than size, including the character, location and design of the school, the quality of teaching, and the way it is managed. Both large and small schools can be well or poorly managed. There are many high performing schools in Australia with large enrolments, for instance, but a closer look will generally show that they are structured and organised in such a way that different parts of the school operate as smaller discrete entities.

Any generic claim made for the superiority of either small or large schools by virtue of their size should be regarded with suspicion. Size alone is not as important as the ethos of the school, how it is structured and managed, and the quality of teaching.

Teacher attributes

All available evidence points beyond doubt to quality teaching as the mainstay of an excellent school. Teacher quality has many dimensions – recruitment, pre-service education, graduation standards, induction, professional learning, retention and evidence-based practice – and all have a positive connection with high performance.

> All available evidence points beyond doubt to quality teaching as the mainstay of an excellent school. Teacher quality has many dimensions – recruitment, pre-service education, graduation standards, induction, professional learning, retention and evidence-based practice – and all have a positive connection with high performance.

As many countries that have chosen to prioritise teacher quality in their quest for a better education system can attest, it takes time and resources to raise the quality of the teaching workforce. Finland's celebrated education success from the time PISA testing began in 2000 rests heavily on reforms set in train in 1979 which focused on the teaching workforce. For some time now, Finland has typically recruited teachers from the highest achieving cohort of graduates and has trained them vigorously, with a focus on classroom practice. Finnish teacher training programs are distinguished by their depth, scope, and academic challenge. All teachers have undergraduate and master's degrees from a research university, and subject specialists earn their master's degree from the university's academic departments. A demanding quality standard is applied at graduation. Although teacher salaries are not high in comparison with other OECD countries, teaching is an esteemed profession in Finland.

While Finland has slipped back in the rankings in recent PISA cycles, it remains a high performing country and explanations for its declining levels of achievement, apart from its ranking against other countries, do not suggest any diminution of teacher quality. They refer instead to social and economic change outside the school, including an increased number of immigrant students in schools, changes in the curriculum, less time spent in school, and changes in resource distribution, with some municipalities having cut spending and merged schools. Commentators on Finland's changing PISA results observe that while teacher quality is measurably important – even dominant – in its contribution to high student performance, it does not stand alone. There are still other important components of schooling with a strong influence on achievement, and there are also students and families to consider.

Like Finland, Singapore's outstanding success in recent PISA cycles has been attributed in large part to its decision to make teacher quality, along with the curriculum, a centrepiece of its education reforms in the 1990s. Over two decades, the quality of teachers in Singapore has been boosted by a suite of deliberate policies designed to increase the status and prestige of the profession. Entrants to teacher training are selected from the top 30% of school leavers and graduates, and candidates are accepted only after an interview assessing their commitment and suitability. Teacher education students are supported by generous stipends through their training and teachers receive high salaries. Teacher education is conducted by the one academically rigorous institution, the National Institute for Education, which receives on average 16,000 applications for 2,000 places. Singapore has purposefully accepted large class sizes of 30 to 40 students rather than increasing teacher numbers and recognises and rewards expertise in a teaching career.

Recognition of the key importance of quality teaching to student outcomes has led to a raft of reviews and inquiries into teacher quality in Australia over two decades and the introduction of standards for initial teacher education programs and for graduating teachers. These many reviews and new standards have had little discernible impact on recruitment into the profession or on teacher education programs. At the beginning of each university year, the media voices widely shared concerns about the poor end-of-school results accepted by universities for school-leavers entering teacher education programs, with prospective teachers having on average the lowest ATAR scores of all university entrants. In comparison with other high performing PISA countries, Australia has the highest share of low achievers in university teacher education programs, and one of the lowest shares of high achievers. Teaching in Australia attracts only a small proportion of high achieving school leavers.

Most initial teacher education in Australian universities is conducted in Bachelor of Education programs rather than academic faculties, casting doubt on the strength of the academic credentials of content-specific teachers. With so many different programs offered in Australian universities, questions necessarily persist about the varying quality of provision. Measures have found that a teacher's university qualifications can be important, especially for teaching in the upper years of schooling. Analysis of PISA data shows that teachers with a master's degree increase the rate of learning of students by 20%, and those with a PhD by 80%. According to PISA and TIMSS contextual data, Australia has a smaller than average proportion of teachers with a postgraduate qualification, even compared with those countries which do not require a postgraduate qualification for entry to the profession.

> Beyond degree qualification however, teachers' content knowledge and subject matter expertise also influence outcomes.

Beyond degree qualification however, teachers' content knowledge and subject matter expertise also influence outcomes. The most effective teachers have a deep understanding of the subjects they teach and if this deep knowledge falls below a certain level, it can have detrimental effects. Hence the importance of the extent of 'out of field' teaching, teachers without qualifications, knowledge and expertise in their subject area, specifically maths and science, or primary teachers without adequate literacy and numeracy skills. Countries with a lot of secondary teachers teaching 'out of field' perform poorly in PISA, TIMSS and PIRLS. Australia has a substantial proportion of teachers, especially teachers of STEM subjects – science, technology, engineering and maths – teaching 'out-of-field', partly because of the large number of small secondary schools in Australia that are widely dispersed geographically. 'Out of field' teaching is more common in the lower years of secondary schooling than the senior years, understandably to allow qualified staff to be assigned to the more academically demanding senior classes, but with the result that some students will be discouraged early on from continuing their STEM studies.

Starting salaries for teachers in Australia are quite high by international standards and in comparison with other graduate entry professions, but teachers reach the top of the salary scale relatively quickly so do not retain the salary advantage over their career, nor is there financial reward for teaching excellence. Policies over the past twenty years have given preference to reducing class size over raising salaries.

While the science of measuring teacher effectiveness is necessarily inexact and is confounded by the many other factors that influence achievement, some measurements have been made of the impact a good teacher can make. Parents understandably expect that their child will make a year's progress for each year in school, yet research shows that there will be a significant difference in the performance of students with more or less effective teachers. One measure, based on PISA results, suggests that a highly effective teacher can make a difference of up to a year in a student's progress, with the differences being more evident in reading than in maths. On this calculation, it has been estimated that an average student, on the 50th percentile of achievement, would rise to somewhere between the 79th and 95th percentile with a more effective teacher. Added to this is the impact good teachers have on non-cognitive traits such as respect, caring, effort and motivation, the range of attributes which are impossible to measure but equally important in achieving excellence and as an outcome of schooling in themselves.

Teacher effects are more marked in primary school, possibly because at this stage of schooling, students spend most of their time with one class teacher. The effects have been found to be additive and cumulative in the primary school years where the basic skills of literacy and numeracy are the foundation for further learning. They diminish over time. Studies have shown that students who are assigned to several ineffective teachers in a row in primary school have significantly lower achievement and fewer gains in achievement than those who are assigned to highly effective teachers in sequence. This has been measured as a 52 percentile difference in scores after three years for students with comparable abilities.

> ...the research evidence on the paramount importance of teacher effectiveness is overwhelming, and accords with most people's experience of school, as students and as parents.

Research on teacher effectiveness at secondary school confirms that students with more effective teachers score significantly higher in standard tests, but the cumulative effect observed in primary school is no longer evident for secondary students. In secondary school, students in classes with highly effective teachers perform at a high level, regardless of the effectiveness of their previous teacher, while students who previously had an effective teacher are seen to experience a learning setback with a less effective teacher.

While the metrics may be inexact, the research evidence on the paramount importance of teacher effectiveness is overwhelming, and accords with most people's experience of school, as students and as parents. A signal of a good school is the value it places on its teachers, its commitment to recruiting high quality staff and developing teacher expertise. There is a large volume of research indicating the characteristics to be found in the most effective teachers: they will have graduated from a high quality teacher education program and will engage in continuing professional development; generalist primary teachers will have high threshold levels of knowledge of literacy, numeracy and science as well as pedagogy while specialist subject teachers will have thorough content knowledge in their field; effective teachers will have a good knowledge of assessment and how to use it to remediate and extend their students and will understand the power of feedback; they will have the capacity to use a range of teaching strategies for different students; they will know their students well, build positive relationships with them and set high expectations for all, expecting every student to succeed; and they will have the skills to manage the classroom environment and will collaborate with colleagues. Teacher enthusiasm is also important – teachers who support students and are enthusiastic about their teaching get the best results.

As is evident from this list, beyond qualifications and experience, it is the way teachers practise their profession – the skills they have in adapting their teaching to the needs of their students – that defines effective teaching. Increasingly, teacher professionalism is given weight as a way of increasing both the attractiveness and effectiveness of teaching. In high performing systems, teachers are 'informed professionals', using research, data and information and the skills and judgement they have learned in their training to inform their practice, cooperating with their colleagues in the interests of their students. Greater teacher professionalism, where teachers are given more scope to teach within the framework of a demanding curriculum, more authority for managing student behaviour, and more time for interpreting assessment results, preparing lessons, collaborating with colleagues and using support staff effectively, is associated with improved performance.

Not only do effective teachers increase student learning, they also enhance children's experience of school. The evidence shows that when students have good relations with their teachers, both their performance and their sense of belonging at school benefit. A positive attitude to school, nurtured by a supportive and encouraging teacher who sets high expectations, is associated with high performance.

> Not only do effective teachers increase student learning, they also enhance children's experience of school.

Teacher practice – the curriculum, and how it's delivered

Quality teaching practice is inextricably linked with the content of schooling, as embodied in the curriculum and its delivery, assessment and reporting. While the more measurable teacher attributes of academic qualifications, preparation and participation in professional development are headlined as indicators of teacher quality, curriculum content and how teachers deliver it are equally important.

The importance of the curriculum comes from its role in determining what is taught, when, and to what standard. Its power lies in setting expectations and standards for what students will learn and be able to do at each stage of schooling. According to the research, a high quality curriculum will set clear expectations of progress and will demand high standards. It will emphasise both substantive content knowledge and essential competencies such as critical thinking, problem solving, effective communication, and accessing and analysing information. It will not be too crowded or too prescriptive. And it will be aligned with assessment, to enable diagnosis of each student's learning needs.

> According to the research, a high quality curriculum will set clear expectations of progress and will demand high standards.

Analysis of PISA results so far have not led to proposals about the ideal content of the school curriculum, but the data consistently show the benefits of setting high standards, the need for teachers to be expert in their content area, and the necessity of structured and organised teaching. Where expectations are low, so is performance.

System-wide curriculum documents generally leave abundant scope for interpretation and choice of materials at the classroom level, hence the paramount importance of teaching skills. The effectiveness of a curriculum depends on the way it is translated into the classroom and this comes back to the approaches and strategies teachers use to implement it. No matter how ambitious and demanding a curriculum is, its impact will always be limited by how well it is delivered.

The Australian federal system, whereby states and territories have responsibility for what happens in schools, means that the Australian Curriculum, designed for the ten years of schooling up to the senior secondary years, is even more removed from what happens in the classroom than most national curriculum documents. The Australian Curriculum is translated into schools and classrooms by state and territory school authorities, who provide their own curriculum resources, and by schools and teachers themselves. Each of the two largest states, New South Wales and Victoria, incorporate the Australian Curriculum into state based curriculum documents.

Achieving a proper balance between content and process is key, yet the process of teaching is beset by an ideological divide which could be resolved by considering the evidence on how learning occurs. Debate about the nature of the school curriculum in Australia and elsewhere often falls into two camps, with advocates for student centred, inquiry-based teaching labelled 'progressive,' and those supporting an approach involving the teaching of facts and knowledge in goal-oriented classes based on the curriculum labelled 'conservative'. As with most issues, the political labels are unhelpful and the answer lies somewhere in between, finding a balance between knowledge-based, teacher-directed learning and problem-solving, student-led learning for particular students, with teachers being able to adapt their teaching accordingly. The best outcomes come from choosing the right approach at the right time.

The supposed dichotomy between teacher-directed and student-led learning is exemplified by the 'reading wars', a long-running debate in Australia and overseas about the teaching of reading, specifically concerning the adoption of an explicit or direct teaching approach involving skills such as phonics and phonemic awareness, as opposed to 'whole language' teaching. The evidence clearly supports an approach which incorporates phonics and phoneme awareness as an essential component in teaching reading, most especially to children at risk of reading failure, but does not eschew the need to develop other aspects of literacy development such as fluency, vocabulary and comprehension through other approaches. The introduction of a Year 1 Phonics Check in some schools in Australia and overseas has been designed to assess students' ability to decode letters and sounds at a critical point in their reading development. In the United Kingdom, where a Phonics Check was implemented nationally in 2012, there is solid evidence of improvements in reading, as there is also in Australian states which have trialled a Phonics Check.

Regular reviews of the curriculum are generally fraught with this kind of polarised positioning. A 2021 revision of the elementary school curriculum in Alberta, Canada – the highest performing Canadian province in PISA – characterised as 'knowledge-rich', with a strong focus on 'evidence, numeracy and literacy', has been criticised on political and ideological grounds for its 'heavy load of factual information.' At the time of writing, a review of the Australian Curriculum was under way (it was completed in early 2022). The review addressed concerns about the lack of ambition and high standards in the curriculum, its failure to set a strong foundation of knowledge as a platform for future learning and the politicisation of certain content areas such as history. The mathematics component in particular has been criticised for diluting and delaying the acquisition of content knowledge and basic skills and for emphasising open-ended inquiry without the systematic building of coherent knowledge which is a prerequisite to inquiry and problem solving. Getting the balance right is a challenging business.

The evidence underlines the need for a strong component of teacher-led learning at certain stages of schooling. Hattie's analysis of hundreds of studies of effective teaching practice concludes that active, guided instruction is more than three times as effective as the unguided, student-led teaching that is associated with constructivist practices. PISA and TIMSS results come to the same conclusion. PISA results show the benefits of targeted teaching – student achievement is greater where teachers are more likely to provide individual help when students have difficulties. TIMSS results show that more frequent use of direct instructional approaches has a positive effect on students' maths performance. Targeted teaching strategies, where teachers use different approaches to teaching students with different levels of ability, contribute to better outcomes. In the PISA science results from 2018, for example, higher performance levels are achieved where students report stronger teacher explanation. Teacher explanation is associated with confident teaching and teacher quality, while its converse, free investigation by students, is associated with unorganised teaching and teacher's lack of coherent and confident content knowledge, and with lower achievement levels.

> *The evidence underlines the need for a strong component of teacher-led learning at certain stages of schooling.*

Backing up the data from education analysis, the science of cognition shows that, in terms of human brain development, content and knowledge are needed as a foundation for developing skills and values. Cognitive science, the study of the mind and intelligence, shows how the brain uses and stores knowledge, demonstrating that knowledge is a necessary prerequisite for exploration, problem solving and creative and critical thinking. Knowledge also leads to curiosity and motivation and hence higher attainment. Deeper thinking skills need domain-specific content on which to work; you cannot use these skills unless you have something to think about. Learning is sequential. It is only when students master enough foundational knowledge that they can fully benefit from inquiry-based learning.

In the interests of learning from high performing education systems, it has been popular to look at Finland, which has identified as a bedrock of its success a curriculum framework that was not prescriptive about the details of what to teach and how to teach but relied heavily on its high quality teaching profession having the capacity to develop curriculum and conduct diagnostic assessments themselves. Observers of classroom practice in Finland have noted however that practice in schools differed from the curriculum policy framework as officially described. Despite the overall policy approach, in their classrooms, teachers continued until quite recently to use traditional structured direct teaching approaches. More recent Finnish reforms have explicitly rejected traditional instruction in favour of a 'phenomenon based' approach, which breaks down subject-based compartmentalisation of knowledge and, instead of focusing on a specific subject such as mathematics, literacy or history, explores phenomena across subject boundaries. The approach is said to promote problem-based inquiry and more personalised learning. At the same time, analysis of Finland's recent international testing results draws attention to the over-use of self-directed learning practices and digital learning materials as one of several reasons for its decline in absolute performance as well as a decline in its international ranking.

The evidence that it is typically the specific classroom rather than the school that makes the most difference to student outcomes highlights the significance of individual teaching practice in driving student outcomes. In most PISA-participating countries, achievement differences within schools are far greater than differences between schools, and it is variation in teacher effectiveness that is the strongest in-school determinant of those differences. Analysis of PISA and TIMSS maths scores for Australia show that variations in teaching practice are the most significant explanation for the differences that are reported here.

It is common to question the relevance to Australia of the high PISA performance of East Asian education systems on the basis of their reputation for 'hothouse schooling', their rigorous, coherent systematic curricula, characterised by academic rigour, explicit teaching and repeated practice by students, with highly scripted classrooms and a heavy focus on exams. If that were an apt characterisation of those systems today, students from those regions would not excel in the PISA tests, as PISA does not test knowledge per se but measures how well 15 year-olds can problem solve and apply their analytical knowledge and skills to real world situations. Singapore attributes its recent success in PISA in part to the curriculum reform it has been pursuing since the 1990s alongside improvements in teacher quality. Recent reforms in Singapore and other East Asian countries have seen a shift towards more problem-solving, creativity and innovation, based on a strong foundation of mastery first of basic skills and knowledge. In these countries, while there are moves to lessen dependence on rote learning, repetitive tests and a 'one size fits all' type of instruction and to foster more differentiated teaching and greater student engagement, problem-solving is still built on initial curriculum content that is very demanding in terms of fluency in basic skills and concepts. A strong knowledge base is regarded as an essential foundation. The slogan "Teach Less, Learn More" captures the essence of this shift in Singapore, exemplifying the same approach of quality over quantity adopted in relation to teaching.

Assessment

PISA has also highlighted the need for coherence between curriculum, standards and assessment. For teachers, assessment is an integral part of their teaching and their students' learning, a means of identifying the progress and learning needs of individual students. Its educational purpose is primarily diagnostic, to assess individual student learning needs so that teachers can adapt their teaching to meet them. Teachers' skills in formative assessment, which enables them to support students' progress, and in summative assessment, which allows them to judge students' performance at the end of a program of work, are critical. Increasingly teachers and schools need the skills to analyse and use the data that come from assessment – both their own assessments and system-wide data such as NAPLAN – to inform their teaching. By using good data and interpreting it well, a teacher is in a position to have an informed conversation with each student about where they are, where they want to go and how they might get there.

Alongside teacher quality, an important success factor in Finnish education is considered to be the systematic approach taken to identifying individual student needs and addressing them, relying on teachers' skills in diagnosis and assessment to single out students needing special support. Close collaboration between classroom teachers and special teachers means that extra support is provided when it is needed. As a result, a large proportion of Finnish students are given personalised attention to address diagnosed learning needs throughout their schooling, especially in the primary years. On one recent measure, almost half the Finnish students completing compulsory education at age 16 had received special education attention at some point in their schooling.

The design of assessment processes is critical. In analysing PISA results, the OECD has noted the limitations of certain types of assessment used in schools and school systems, such as multiple choice tests and basic proficiency testing, observing that assessment processes in high performing education systems focus on the acquisition of complex, higher-order thinking skills, and the application of those skills to problems students have never seen before. The most informative assessment, it is said, relies little on multiple choice computer-scored tests as these cannot measure problem-solving skills and make limited cognitive and meta-cognitive demands on students.

PISA data also show the value of end-of-school external examinations, examinations that define performance relative to an external standard, not relative to other students in the classroom or school. In countries where standards-based external exams are conducted, they are associated with the higher performance of school systems, although it is not at all clear that the link is causal, nor are they considered to be a main driver of achievement. Even Finland, which has claimed the eschewing of standardised assessments as a factor in its education success, has maintained its externally administered, high stakes matriculation examination at the end of high school as a measure of academic achievement and to determine entry into university. Studies in federations such as Canada and Germany where different assessment systems exist have also found achievement gains for those provinces/states with external exit exams.

> PISA data also show the value of end-of-school external examinations...

The main benefit of external examinations, according to research, is the incentive they provide for high achievement, and the opportunity for all to excel. Without them, there is little recognition or reward for academic excellence. As long as university entry is relatively easy, students have no incentive to take hard subjects, or perform at the highest possible level. Generally, the performance gains are found to be greater for higher ability students. In the absence of external assessment, the incentive for high achievement, where it exists, is either individually motivated or comes from parents or the school.

Technology

One element of schooling, and everyday life, which attracts a mixed reaction is the use of technology in the classroom, by teachers and students. Many countries make significant investments in technologies in schools, expecting a transformative effect, yet evidence about the value of these investments is unclear, tending towards a less than glowing report on their impact on performance. This was the case at least before COVID-19 forced an even greater reliance on technologies as students all over the world spent months or longer learning at home. Research into the performance of students in 2020 and 2021 will likely show significant learning benefits from a range of educational technologies, with different results depending on students' access to technology, and teachers' skills in deploying it. For the present, however, the report card is mixed.

> Data from PISA 2018 show that the more digital tools are used in lessons, the worse the learning outcomes. Analysis indicates that digital distraction is now an issue for most countries.

Data from PISA 2018 show that the more digital tools are used in lessons, the worse the learning outcomes. Analysis indicates that digital distraction is now an issue for most countries. Students everywhere it seems are easily distracted by the devices themselves and use them for other than schoolwork. While moderate screen time (2 to 4 hours a day outside school) is shown to have a positive effect, there is a clear adverse impact on performance when students spend more time outside school on a screen. Digital devices however are just one component of the educational technology armoury.

The main conclusion from pre COVID-19 research studies is that some technologies such as screens and social media can be harmful, especially if over-used, and that technology works best when it is integrated with the curriculum and when it is in the hands of teachers rather than students. PISA 2018 analysis highlights the importance of students gaining the knowledge and understanding to make sense of the vast information bank to which technology gives them easy access. Across PISA-participating countries, fewer than one in ten students was able to distinguish between fact and opinion when reading about an unfamiliar topic, pointing to the need for schools to build up the skills students need to navigate their way through online resources and assess the validity and trustworthiness of the information they come across.

Behaviour

Teachers' skills in managing the classroom environment have been found to be an important factor driving student outcomes. Classroom discipline is a core element of effective teaching, directly impacting on achievement. When classrooms are noisy and disorderly, when disruptive student behaviour is not managed and when lesson time is lost while the class settles down, student achievement is negatively affected. Both PISA and TIMSS results show that the better the classroom disciplinary climate, the more time is spent on teaching and learning and the stronger is student performance, underlining the importance of teachers' skills in managing behaviour.

> *Australian schools have been found to have one of the weakest classroom disciplinary climates...*

Class order and cohesion is an important explanation for variations in performance, especially at the high school level. In analysis of PISA results, Australian schools have been found to have one of the weakest classroom disciplinary climates, with teachers here having to spend more time maintaining order than most other participating countries. In PISA 2018, PIRLS 2016 and TIMSS 2019, compared with the average, Australia had more frequent bullying in school, despite the existence of clear school policies on bullying, Australian students were more likely to have skipped school, and a higher than average proportion of Australian students reported disrupted classrooms, measured as the time teachers have to wait for students to quieten down. These differences in disciplinary climate are more apparent within than between schools, highlighting again the importance of individual classroom and teacher characteristics, and are clearly associated with differences in performance. Achievement is demonstrably higher in schools with fewer disciplinary and safety problems and with less bullying.

A general orderly atmosphere is recognised as an important characteristic of an effective school, just as an orderly well-managed class is associated with better outcomes for students. PISA and TIMSS use indicators such as the disciplinary climate, students' sense of belonging, degree of teacher support and a culture of high expectations for all to show how higher performance is associated with an orderly and cooperative environment, a sense of belonging at school, greater support from teachers, and having meaningful goals, high standards and ambitious learning.

School ethos

Possibly the least measurable of the many components of school quality is the amorphous concept of the ethos or climate of a school, yet this dimension of quality is consistently identified as a key variable both in student performance and in student well-being. A positive school climate may be difficult to measure, but it is easily recognisable when you see it. For many parents and students, it is this overall impression of a school, their subjective sense of its culture and values and sense of community, their observation of the way students and staff interact, that represents quality. Research studies as well as hard data support this perception as a valid measure of an effective school. A school's climate affects both learning and behaviour. As longitudinal studies show and most adults will attest, a person's experience of schooling has as much of a lasting influence on their success and satisfaction in employment and adult life as their academic results. Longitudinal studies confirm the significant difference a positive school experience can make – young people who enjoyed being at school, enjoyed learning and felt safe and secure are more likely to be doing well post-school regardless of their achievement level. Student well-being stands alongside teaching and learning at the heart of everything a good school does.

Well-being

The school climate appears to have its main effect on student outcomes through its influence on motivational factors such as commitment to school, incentive to learn and student satisfaction, factors which are related to achievement but are also important in shaping life chances. The best schools nurture student well-being by fostering non-cognitive attributes such as values, attitudes and character strengths, including a disposition to learning, resilience, conscientiousness, perseverance, curiosity, optimism and self-control.

> The best schools nurture student well-being by fostering non-cognitive attributes such as values, attitudes and character strengths, including a disposition to learning, resilience, conscientiousness, perseverance, curiosity, optimism and self-control.

The evidence on the importance of these non-cognitive attributes and qualities to achievement in school and beyond comes not only from education research but from other research fields such as neuroscience, psychology and economics. It is clear from the evidence that the physical, social and emotional well-being of students underpins academic achievement and success in life – confident, resilient children with a capacity for emotional intelligence perform better academically and are well placed to develop responsible and satisfying lives.

Analysis of PISA data confirms these findings and supports the view that teaching practices can nurture and promote students' drive, motivation and effort, increasing the chances that they will flourish at school. Students with greater stamina, perseverance and capacity for hard work are more likely to succeed than those who are talented but have little capacity to set ambitious goals for themselves and put effort into achieving them. What the research also shows is that these qualities can be learned and fostered, and that schools as well as families play a powerful role in building these character traits. Teachers who put an emphasis on non-cognitive behaviours detectable in classroom behaviour, like effort, organisation, discipline, attendance, participation, enthusiasm and cooperation, are encouraging better academic performance as well as providing a critical foundation for their students in later life.

Numerous studies point to the role of motivation, which encompasses a range of personality traits such as conscientiousness, orderliness, discipline, organisational ability, dutifulness, persistence and a degree of self-belief, as a factor in academic performance. This knowledge underpins a recent trend in education, widely adopted internationally and in Australia, to encourage the development in students of a 'growth mindset', with the conviction that changing students' and teachers' belief about whether or not intelligence can be changed will improve academic success. An industry of resources, materials, experts, consultancies and professional development has grown up around the idea that you can improve academic success by moving students from a fixed mindset, a belief that intelligence is fixed, to a growth mindset, a belief that intelligence is able to grow. The research underpinning the growth mindsets industry has been convincingly challenged on logical, methodological and empirical grounds, suggesting that a degree of scepticism is warranted towards marketing of courses and materials by the growth mindset industry. Insofar as the label captures the value of schools' fostering the important intrinsic qualities of motivation, confidence, self-knowledge, effort, self-regulation, enthusiasm, perseverance, resilience and enthusiasm for learning, all of which are positively linked with achievement and long-term outcomes in the labour market, it rests on a solid evidence base.

Australian students generally do not show strong motivation or goal-orientation compared with students in other PISA-participating countries, and on measures of a positive school climate, we also rank poorly against comparable countries. Yet these personal characteristics such as motivation, enjoyment of learning and self-confidence, and school-related factors such as high expectations, good student-teacher relationships and a calm, controlled atmosphere are held to be at the heart of the resilience of students from non-English speaking families and socially disadvantaged backgrounds who achieve 'against the odds.'

Schools have a variety of ways to foster these individual characteristics conducive to learning, through teaching practices in individual classrooms to the range of activities offered to students, to the atmosphere and expectations of the school as a whole. Within the classroom, factors such as feedback, which stimulates reflection on learning, acknowledges effort and motivates students, and good relationships between teachers and students, contribute to higher achievement. Feedback that is prompt and timely, clear and specific, accurate and objective will contribute to learning. Good teacher student relationships are important from primary school, where the pattern of engagement that is likely to continue through schooling is set. The evidence shows that students learn more and have fewer disciplinary problems when they feel their teachers take them seriously, when they have a positive and constructive relationship with their teacher and when their classrooms are characterised by mutual respect, empathy, warmth and encouragement.

High expectations

The ethos of a school as a whole is evident in the expectations that are set for student achievement and behaviour. The extent to which a school sets high academic expectations for all students, celebrates success and curiosity, and encourages effort and motivation is a mark of its quality. High expectations for all students are associated with higher performance and a stronger sense of well-being, increased interest in and motivation for lessons, better attendance, more positive school behaviours, and a higher likelihood of completing school. In a school where academic activities and student performance are valued by both students and teachers, where students who do well academically are respected by their peers and honoured by the school community and where teachers set challenging work, students respond positively to goals and work hard to achieve them. Research demonstrates the importance of teachers having high expectations – when teachers hold certain beliefs about the potential academic achievement of their students, this can be confirmed in their students' performance and attitudes to school. Similarly, a lack of challenge and low expectations are associated with low performance.

> *High expectations for all students are associated with higher performance and a stronger sense of well-being...*

Academic streaming

Evidence about the importance of teacher expectations is at the centre of different views about the advantages and disadvantages of academic streaming. Mixed-ability classes are the norm in the early years of schooling in Australia although students may be grouped for specific subjects such as maths or English, on the basis of teacher assessment, to enable more targeted teaching. Streaming is more commonly used for older students, based on their prior achievement. The evidence is inconclusive on the impact of streaming on achievement levels, with the results of studies depending largely on whether the researcher's focus is on high or average performance. General streaming of whole class levels is considered to be disadvantageous, and is not now common, but grouping by ability in particular subjects at secondary school, most obviously in maths and second language learning, is associated in most studies with benefits for academically strong students, but with a possible negative impact on the lowest performers in terms of their motivation and self-esteem. Studies find that with their academic peers, advanced students can move ahead and not be bored, whereas without grouping, teachers tend to 'teach to the middle'. The result though is often that the weakest classes get the weakest teachers.

Cross-country studies have found that individual student achievement is higher than expected in a higher achieving peer group. Research that controls for factors such as family background and school characteristics has found that peer average achievement has a highly significant effect on achievement growth and that students benefit from having higher achieving schoolmates over their school career. Peer group influence on achievement is both positive and cumulative.

One explanation given for this peer group effect is that peers, like family, are a source of motivation and aspiration, as well as providing direct interactions in learning. A particularly significant aspect of these peer group relationships is the incentive and support high achieving fellow students provide for high academic achievement. Peers affect the classroom processes through the pace of teaching, the behaviour of students, and the character of teacher-student interactions. Australian research has suggested a variety of reasons for the higher than expected performance of students in schools with a strong academic ethos: the curriculum and the teaching are delivered at a higher level; the school's and teachers' expectations are higher; students' norms regarding the usefulness of academic work are more conducive to learning; and there is less distraction from teaching and learning.

Single sex schools

One aspect of peer group interaction in schools which is much examined, though without a clear-cut result, is the issue of single sex schooling. The main claims for single sex education are academic, that both boys and girls are more likely to achieve their potential in a single sex environment. Many studies show the benefits in terms of academic attainment and social outcomes to single sex schooling, especially for girls, and many former students of single sex schools attest to their value for them, but it is important to first take the nature of the student body into account. The consensus from impartial research is that single sex education per se brings no advantages, either to examination results or to subject take-up. What matters most in the outstanding final year results of many single sex schools is the academic ability of the students who go there. After that, other features of quality schooling, such as teacher commitment, quality of leadership, parental support and peer group influence have been found to have an important impact.

> ... the evidence shows little academic impact from a single sex education, but in a diverse society, it may be important that the choice is there...

Certainly, the evidence shows little academic impact from a single sex education, but in a diverse society, it may be important that the choice is there, to accommodate different needs. Ultimately the research affirms the critical importance to high achievement, for both boys and girls, of prior ability, high expectations and quality teaching.

Extra-curricular activities

Peer groups are also an important factor in the non-cognitive outcomes of schooling. Research studies on the functioning of peer relationships, especially in adolescence, have demonstrated how peer group norms, values and attitudes can either undermine or facilitate academic achievement. Association with positive peers has been found to play a substantial role in increasing student achievement as well as increasing student engagement and attachment to school. By engaging students in opportunities and activities beyond the classroom, schools demonstrate their commitment to student success and the expectation that all students are able to achieve in a range of domains and pursuits.

Numerous studies, including PISA analysis, point to the importance of structured extra-curricular activities for development and growth, especially during adolescence, and longitudinal studies affirm that the positive effects of extra-curricular participation endure well beyond school. Participation is associated with lower rates of anti-social and risky behaviour, lower rates of academic failure and lower dropout rates.

Explanations for the positive impact of extracurricular activities generally point to the influence of participation on non-cognitive attributes. To some researchers, it is the identification with school and commitment to school-related values – a sense of belonging to the school – that bring the most benefit. To others, it is the improvement in non-cognitive skills such as task persistence, independence, following instructions, working within groups, dealing well with authority figures and fitting in with peers that produces gains in learning. Some researchers point to the important ways in which participation in extra-curricular activities reinforces classroom values, including achievement, independence and peer relationships, thus underlining the focus of schools on student well-being.

The type of activity does not make much difference to these findings, although special claims have been made in research for more direct benefits arising from involvement in school and extra-curricular music. Several research studies have demonstrated powerful effects of music education on personal and academic development, showing that involvement in arts and music programs increases academic achievement, attendance and performance on standardised tests. There is also research to back up claims that "music makes you smarter" by increasing spatial-temporal reasoning skills, encouraging mathematical reasoning, and increasing memory. Many studies have found improvements in numeracy and maths as a result of music education.

More established are the findings that participation in extra-curricular activities of all kinds contributes to student social and emotional well-being, and the non-cognitive qualities that underpin achievement.

Parents, and homework

It is universally accepted that parents' attitudes, behaviours and actions in relation to their children's education have a substantial impact on achievement. Underlining the notion of education as a joint endeavour between school and home, the more parents are engaged with their child's schooling and the more they show the value they place on education, the more they contribute to high performance. Showing an interest in school life, discussing their child's progress with teachers and being involved in school governance or extra-curricular activities all go towards creating a positive learning environment which boosts achievement.

> ...the more parents are engaged with their child's schooling and the more they show the value they place on education, the more they contribute to high performance...

One practical contribution parents make is through their involvement in homework. This involvement is a signal of parents' expectations and aspirations, and the value they place on education. Research evidence on the value of homework is fairly consistent in showing a positive though not large influence on individual student achievement. Homework has different purposes at different stages of schooling, in the early years fostering positive attitudes and habits and reinforcing learning introduced in class, and in higher grades, reinforcing and extending classroom learning. Homework can help struggling students learn material covered in class, help store the material in students' long term memory, and provide additional stimulation for high performers.

Research has found that the nature of homework makes a difference to its value, as does the nature of parent and teacher involvement in it. The impact of homework on achievement is less if parents take a controlling, supervisory approach, and greater when teachers are actively involved, giving timely and relevant feedback.

Secondary students show greater gains from homework than primary students, as the PISA tests of 15 year-olds show. Students who spend more time doing homework tend to score higher in PISA, with each hour of homework translating into higher scores in reading, mathematics and science.

The physical environment

Research on the quality of school facilities generally finds that the physical environment of a school has only a small influence on performance, less than most other dimensions of quality, except insofar as the physical facilities reflect and affect the overall school climate. What is important is not so much the adequacy or design of buildings but the sense they convey of the school culture and morale. A high quality physical environment can foster a strong sense of belonging that is associated in turn with enthusiasm for learning. Poor quality facilities, on the other hand, have an impact on morale at school, the commitment of teachers and students and the willingness of the community to engage. When facilities are inadequate, it appears that the focus on academic achievement is lessened, the school environment is less orderly and serious, and teachers are less likely to show enthusiasm for their work. All these factors contribute to a poor school climate which in turn has its effect on performance.

Beyond their influence on school climate, buildings can affect the comfort of teachers and students. Buildings that are dilapidated, or overcrowded, or too hot or too cold with poor lighting and poorly designed for the purpose, have been found to have a negative influence on student performance. Deficiencies in temperature, lighting, and acoustics adversely impact learning, for obvious reasons.

An appealing and well-maintained school and classroom environment is associated with a positive school climate which fosters student well-being and encourages learning.

School leadership

All these elements of school quality are brought together in the person and role of the school principal and other staff with leadership roles in the school. Leadership, it has been found, drives higher achievement indirectly, by shaping and influencing the culture of a school. The most important element of the principal's role is to set the tone for the school – the school climate – by setting challenging goals, valuing achievement, and fostering a safe collaborative professional environment for teaching, a strong sense of community and common purpose in the school, and an orderly and supportive school environment.

> *The most important element of the principal's role is to set the tone for the school ... by setting challenging goals, valuing achievement, and fostering a safe collaborative professional environment for teaching, a strong sense of community and common purpose in the school, and an orderly and supportive school environment.*

The most effective principals focus on the core business of teaching and learning, and are capable of recognising and inspiring excellence while also challenging and questioning mediocrity. Despite the difficulty of separating the contribution of a principal from other school factors influencing achievement, where measurement has been ventured the evidence suggests that an effective principal can raise the achievement of a typical student in their school by between two and seven months of learning in one school year. An ineffective principal would lower achievement by the same amount. While the principal's impact is measurably less than a teacher's, the difference is that the quality of school leadership affects all students in the school, while the teacher's main impact is on their own classes.

School leadership is where the evidence on quality schooling and the day to day practice in schools ultimately converge. None of the data and evidence rehearsed in this book is new information to educators, nor is any of it counter-intuitive or particularly controversial. School leaders who are aware of the factors that underpin student achievement and well-being and apply this information in their own school context, using their own student data, are in the best position to preside over a high quality school where students will achieve their academic potential and enjoy their years at school.

Part 3
What the latest performance data show

There will always be some concerns about how well schools are doing what is expected of them, a function partly of the many and varied demands made on teachers and schools. No education system will ever perfectly suit everyone or be able to deliver on all objectives for all individual students. Nor is it possible to assess how well schools are meeting expectations in all spheres because many of the objectives of schooling are the shared responsibility of school, family and individual students, and are notoriously difficult to measure or at least to specify causal relationships. In relation to the core business of schools, student learning, there is a wealth of data available to show how Australian students are performing currently, compared with their peers, compared with the past, and compared with other countries. In addition there are volumes of detailed, objective and reliable analysis to hand which put these data into context and explain or at least hypothesise about their links with different elements of schooling.

With so much noise about in the public discourse on education, it is worthwhile being at least generally aware of the data that provide the statistical backdrop to determining the important influences on schooling outcomes. The general summary of several key education data sets which follows presents a recent picture of Australian student performance. This information is in the public domain, and demonstrates outcomes, patterns and trends that are linked with important elements of schooling such as teacher quality, curriculum content and school context.

International data

PISA

The three yearly international PISA surveys test the knowledge and skills of a sample of 15 year-old in the three domains of reading, maths and science. In the past, Australian schools have been rated as 'high performing' and 'high equity'. We have generally ranked well above the OECD average and been in the top tier of high performing countries, in terms of student achievement and in the extent to which our education system is fair and inclusive.

The PISA results from 2018 however show a picture of Australian student achievement in a pattern of decline. Compared with previous performance, Australian students are about a year behind where they were at the turn of the millennium. Relative to other nations too, Australia's performance is declining, to a worrying degree. Over the long term, Australia has one of the most marked declines in performance in all three domains among all PISA-participating countries.

> Over the long term, Australia has one of the most marked declines in performance in all three domains among all PISA-participating countries.

The PISA testing process is managed in Australia by the Australian Council for Educational Research (ACER), which analyses the results statistically and reports them in detail to the public for each PISA cycle. The official reporting of the results is not inclined to a gloomy view of Australian education. The analysis tends to emphasise the positive aspects of the results and, where performance is disappointing, to focus on the link between lower achievement levels and socio-economic disadvantage. With test cycles since 2012 however ACER has headlined its concern about the results. In relation to the 2015 tests for instance ACER announced "Latest PISA Results: Australia at the Crossroads", and for the 2018 tests, 'Australian Student Performance in Long-term

Decline'. Mean performance in all three domains has been steadily declining, from initially high levels of performance, at least in reading and maths, with the steepest decline in maths, a worrying result for a nation that would like to stake its future on science, technology, engineering and maths (STEM) skills.

As always, the devil is in the detail when looking at a large bank of data. While overall average scores are significant, more telling information comes from a closer examination, over time, of different aspects of the results. In the 2018 tests, for the first time in any domain, Australia failed to exceed the OECD average in mathematics. Fourteen countries that had previously performed at a similar or lower level to Australia now outperform us. ACER reported that the decline was such that the average achievement of an Australian 15-year-old in 2018 was, in reading, almost one year of schooling behind a 15-year-old in 2000; in maths, more than one full year of schooling behind a 15-year-old in 2003; and in science, almost one full year of schooling behind a fifteen-year-old in 2006. In 2018, our performance in maths was similar to the OECD average, lower than 23 of the 78 participating countries; in reading and science, our results were lower than 10 and 12 other countries respectively. Where other countries have been improving, Australia has not. As ACER was reported as saying, "This is about much more than 'test-taking' – it's about how well we are preparing Australia's students for adult life."

As mentioned previously, each PISA cycle focuses on a particular skill area. In 2018, this was reading. The ten highest ranking countries in PISA 2018 in reading were, in order, B-S-J-Z China (the four provinces/municipalities of Beijing, Shanghai, Jiangsu and Zhejiang), Singapore, Macao (China), Hong Kong (China), Estonia, Canada, Finland, Ireland, Korea and Poland. Australia was ranked 16th in reading, 29th in maths and 17th in science. Compared with the highest performing region, B-S-J-Z China, Australian students performed at a level roughly one-and-a-half school years lower in reading, around three-and-a-half school years lower in maths, and around three years lower in science. Compared with Singapore, Australian students performed at a level one-and-a-third school years lower in reading, around three years lower in maths, and around one-and-three-quarters of a school year lower in science.

Australia's performance at both the top and the lowest proficiency levels in maths and reading has declined significantly since PISA 2000, with an increase of 7% in the proportion of low performing students and a decline of 4% in performance at the top, in a period where many other countries have seen an increase in the proportion of high performers, alongside a decrease or little change in the proportion of low performers. In maths, 10% of Australian students were high performers, close to the PISA average of 11% and well below the proportion of high achievers in high performing countries such as Singapore (37%) and Canada (15%). The share of low achievers in maths for Australia, at 22%, was also just under the PISA average of 24% and much higher than in high performing countries including Singapore (7%) and Canada (17%). In reading, 13% of Australian students were high performers, compared with the PISA average of 9%, and Singapore's 26% and Canada's 15%. Twenty per cent of Australian students were low performers in reading, against the PISA average of 23%, and 11% for Singapore and 14% for Canada. The proportion of low achieving students in Australia has increased in all three domains. Australia has one of the largest score differences between the top 10% of students and the bottom 10% in reading and in science among PISA-participating countries. A country's share of high and low achievers in PISA has huge ramifications for future economic growth, with a large share of high achievers signalling a skill base for technological advances and innovation, and a high proportion of low achieving students associated with greater unemployment and slower economic growth.

Gender differences in performance among Australian students are similar to the OECD average. Here as elsewhere, girls continue to outperform boys in reading, by the equivalent of about one year of schooling, though boys' performance has remained fairly steady since 2009 while girls' performance has declined. Boys outperformed girls in maths, although the scores for both boys and girls have declined over time, while boys and girls performed similarly in science, with scores for both boys and girls having declined to a similar extent. While the gender gap in maths performance in Australia in favour of male students had been closed in 2015, it reappeared in 2018.

Although on average across the OECD, socio-economic status is a strong predictor of PISA performance, it is noteworthy that for Australian students, the association is weaker than the OECD average, and Australia is numbered among the countries having impressive outcomes for socially disadvantaged students. Australia has a larger percentage of top performers in reading among socio-economically disadvantaged students than most other PISA-participating countries. In reading, family background explains 10% of the variance in performance in Australia, compared with the OECD average of 12%. In maths, it explains 11% of the variation in student performance in Australia compared with 14% on average across the OECD, and in science, 10% against 13%. In reading, some 13% of disadvantaged students in Australia were able to score in the top quarter of performance, compared with 11% OECD average. It is telling that in reading, Australian students classified as most socially advantaged outperformed their most disadvantaged peers by the equivalent of almost three years of schooling, only slightly less than the PISA average. Differences on this scale have remained fairly constant since PISA 2000, with results declining for students in all four socio-economic quartiles, but with the largest decline among the socially advantaged.

> *Australia is numbered among the countries having impressive outcomes for socially disadvantaged students.*

In the OECD's analysis of PISA 2018, Australia is commended, along with Canada and Sweden, for our success in educating students with a migrant background. Australia has a larger than average proportion of students with a migrant background – 28%, compared with the OECD average of 13%. First generation migrant students here performed better in reading than both overseas-born and Australian-born students. Here 29% of immigrant students performed at the top level of reading, compared with 17% across OECD countries on average. The key to making a difference for children from a migrant background is seen to lie mainly in language and social support in school and quality early childhood education, approaches which the evidence suggest have been honed in Australia with its high migrant intake and longstanding multicultural education policies.

The PISA results presented nationally conceal varied outcomes for different states and territories. South Australia, Tasmania and the Northern Territory fell below the OECD average, the ACT and Western Australia both performed better than the average, and New South Wales, Victoria and Queensland met the average. This relative position of the states is fairly consistent, over time and in different testing regimes.

Australia has one of the lowest between-school variations in performance in the PISA tests, and one of the highest within-school variations. High and low performing students in PISA here are spread across schools rather than clustered in particular schools. Between-school variation in Australia is about 20%, against the PISA average of 29%, while the within-school variation is well above the average of 71%. This underlines the evidence that socio-economic differences and disparities between schools are less important than classroom factors, teacher quality and school climate and points to the need to pay more attention to these school-related factors rather than to look for solutions in the level and distribution of resources.

> Australia has one of the lowest between-school variations in performance in the PISA tests, and one of the highest within-school variations.

TIMSS

Just to prove how contrary even solid data can be, the results from the 2019 Trends in International Mathematics and Science Study (TIMSS) paint a more positive picture of Australian student achievement than PISA, although not a completely rosy one. The explanation for the difference may well lie in differences between the tests, with TIMSS being more curriculum focused, and testing younger students. PISA tests in Australia are administered to Year 9 students, while TIMSS tests students in grades 4 and 8.

The results from the 2019 TIMSS tests show improvements over the previous test in 2015 in Year 8 maths and science and Year 4 science, but not in Year 4 maths. In presenting the 2015 results however, the ACER which manages TIMSS and PIRLS testing as well as PISA drew attention to a 20-year slide in maths and science learning, labelling it "a national challenge". Over the seven test cycles since 1995, Australia's average performance in maths and science has improved, but this improvement occurred mainly between 1995 and 2007. The 2019 results show a flat lining of primary school maths results in most states and a slide in average achievement levels in secondary schools in contrast with performance in many other countries.

> In presenting the 2015 results however, the ACER which manages TIMSS and PIRLS testing as well as PISA drew attention to a 20-year slide in maths and science learning, labelling it "a national challenge".

In the 2019 tests, Australia was in the top 10 of the 64 countries participating in TIMSS in Year 8 maths and science and Year 4 science. In Year 4 maths however, which could be seen as a harbinger of future performance, achievement has remained the same for the past three cycles, and Australia was outperformed by 22 countries. In contrast to Australia, most of the other countries which have participated in several cycles of TIMSS have seen their results improve. The highest performing countries, including

Singapore at the top and several other East Asian countries, were a long way ahead of Australia.

The TIMSS results are reported against four benchmarks: Advanced (625 points); High (550 points); Intermediate (475 points); and Low (400 points), and in relation to the proportion of students reaching the National Proficiency Standard, which is set at the Intermediate benchmark. Between 68% and 78% of Australian students achieved the TIMSS Intermediate benchmark or higher, compared with more than 90% of students in Singapore, the highest achieving country. Australian students' average score in Year 4 maths was 516, 110 points behind Singapore and 51 points behind the highest achieving European country, the Russian Federation; in Year 8 maths it was 517, 100 points below Singapore and 26 points below the Russian Federation; in Year 4 science, it was 533, 60 points below Singapore and 34 points behind the Russian Federation; and in Year 8 science, it was 528, 80 points below Singapore and 15 points below the Russian Federation.

The improvement in Australia's average performance in 2019 over 2015 in Year 8 maths and Year 4 and Year 8 Science was mainly due to an increase in the proportion of high performing students. In its numbers of very high performers however Australia still lags behind other countries. In Year 8 maths, 11% of Australian students were very high performers, compared with 51% of students in Singapore. In Year 4 maths, 10% of Australian students were very high performers, compared with 54% of students in Singapore. In Year 4 and Year 8 maths, 10% of Australian students were very low performers, compared with 0% and 2% of students in Singapore. This persistent long tail of underachievement among Australian students is a cause for concern, as is the lag in the proportion of very high performers.

No significant differences can be seen between boys and girls in Year 8 maths or Year 4 or Year 8 science, though boys outperformed girls in Year 4 maths, mainly because of the higher proportion of high performing male students compared with girls. The proportion of boys and girls who attained the national proficiency standard (475 score points) in Year 4 maths is about the same for girls and boys in Australia (69% and 70%), though much lower than the proportion of students achieving that level in Singapore (90%). The proportion of very high performing boys in Year 4 maths (12%) was significantly higher than the proportion of girls (8%) who achieved at this level.

In TIMSS, students from a migrant background achieved at the same level as non-migrant Australian students in Year 4 maths and Year 8 science. In Year 8 maths, students who spoke a language other than English at home outperformed Australian students from an English speaking background, with a markedly higher proportion of very high performing students (26%, compared with 10%) coming from a non-English speaking background. The opposite was true in Year 4 science – students from an English speaking household performed better than students from a non-English speaking background, though the proportions of very high performing students were similar (12% and 9% respectively).

The good TIMSS results nationally for Year 8 students in maths were achieved on the back of significantly improved results in New South Wales. New South Wales, the ACT and Victoria had the highest average scores (534, 521 and 515 respectively), the highest proportion of very high performers (18%, 9% and 11% respectively) and the lowest proportion of very low performers (9%, 6% and 9%). The proportion of students reaching the national proficiency standard in Year 4 science and Year 4 maths varied among states, from a high ACT result of 88% of students in science and 80% of students in maths to a low result in the Northern Territory of 55% of students in science and 46% of students in maths.

PIRLS

While the 2018 PISA results showed a steady decline in reading for Australian 15 year olds, the reading scores of the Year 4 students tested in the Progress in International Reading Literacy Study (PIRLS) in 2016 showed improvement over the scores from 2011, the first year that Australia participated in the program, although our relative position internationally did not improve significantly. In 2011, Australia ranked 27th out of 50 participating countries, with an average score of 527. In 2016, our ranking improved to 21st, and our average score increased to 544, which was significantly lower than 13 other countries, similar to 12 countries, and significantly higher than 24 countries. The high performing countries in PIRLS are similar to those performing well in PISA and TIMSS, with the Russian Federation and Singapore at the top, with average scores of 581 and 576 respectively, and Hong Kong, Ireland, Northern Ireland, England, Finland, and Poland also highly ranked.

In PIRLS as in TIMSS, performance is measured at four levels: Advanced (625 points); High (550 points): Intermediate (475 points); and Low (260 points). The average achievement of Australian students therefore fell between the Intermediate (classified as proficient) and High benchmarks. Only 16% of Australian students performed at the Advanced level (compared with 29% in Singapore), 35% at the High level (compared with 37% in Singapore) and 30% at the Intermediate level (compared with 23% in Singapore). Australia's better overall performance in 2016 is the result of improvement at the higher end of achievement, but a long tail of underperformance persists, with about 20% of students either failing to reach the Low benchmark or being a low performer. In the high performing countries, very few students failed to reach the low benchmark (1% and 3%, for the Russian Federation and Singapore), with only a small proportion of students in these countries (5% and 8%) being low performers.

Similar to the PISA results for reading, almost all countries participating in PIRLS 2016 showed significant differences in reading achievement favouring girls. The difference in Australia between boys' and girls' scores was 22 points, close to the international average difference of 19 points. A higher proportion of girls reached the High and Advanced benchmarks, while more boys than girls were at or below the Low benchmark. These gender differences did not change significantly between 2011 and 2016.

As in PISA, a proxy measure used to determine socio-economic status in PIRLS is a measure of home resources for learning, including the number of books in a home and parents' education level and occupation. Generally, PIRLS confirms other evidence showing at the population level a powerful positive connection between socio-economic background and student achievement, although in Australia the significance of socio-economic status was again less than the average for participating countries. In PIRLS on average, students with many home resources scored 63 points higher than students with some home resources, and 160 points higher than those with few home resources. A high proportion of Australian students, 46%, were classified as having many resources in the home, compared with the average for all countries of 20%. The average score for Australian students with many home resources was 592, 51 points higher than the average for students classified as having only some resources. Only a small proportion of all students – 7% on average for all countries, and 1% of Australian students – were classified as having few resources in the home.

Unlike the PISA and TIMSS results, in PIRLS Australian students from a non-English speaking home background scored on average 15 points lower than students who spoke English at home, reflecting the nature of the test and the age of students participating.

Among the states and territories, Victoria and the ACT recorded the best results, with mean scores of 560 and 552 respectively and having the highest proportions of students meeting the Advanced benchmark (19% and 20%) and the lowest proportion of low performers (14% and 18%). The states with the poorest results and the highest proportion of low performing students were South Australia and the Northern Territory – both had average scores of 527, with 26% and 25% low performers and only 11% and 14% high performers. Western Australia, Queensland and Victoria showed the most improvement between 2011 and 2016, with the other jurisdictions showing no significant change.

Australian data – readiness for school

The earliest metric applied universally to Australian children is the measure of school readiness from the Australian Early Development Census (AEDC), conducted for Australian governments by the Social Research Centre in Melbourne at three-yearly intervals on children as they start full-time school. This measure of school readiness, the product of a mix of individual, family and community factors over a child's first five years, is strongly associated with how well they do in primary school. Children who arrive at school "ready" are more likely to do well.

> *Children who arrive at school "ready" are more likely to do well.*

The home environment is especially significant for a child's language and cognitive development, one of the five domains assessed in the AEDC, and most Australian children are fortunate to get a good start in this respect. Survey data show that most Australian children (79%) were regularly read to or told stories by a parent. As knowledge about the benefits of reading to young children has increased over recent years, so has the proportion of children read to or told stories. Evidence shows that whatever their socio-economic background, young children whose parents read to them regularly and those with more books in the home have higher levels of achievement in the early primary years. Attendance at quality pre-school programs also has a positive association with later school achievement.

At the time of writing, the most recently reported data from the AEDC comes from assessments administered in 2018. The AEDC results are reported as a percentage of children who are considered to be "developmentally on track", "developmentally at risk", or "developmentally vulnerable" in each of five key domains known to be closely linked to child health, education and social outcomes – <u>language and cognitive skills,</u> <u>communication skills and general knowledge,</u> <u>emotional maturity,</u> <u>social competence,</u> and <u>physical health and well-being</u>. The 2018 results suggest that a smaller proportion of children starting school are vulnerable to underachievement than in the previous three Census collections.

This positive trend is apparent in all five developmental domains. Between 2009 and 2018, the percentage of children "developmentally on track" in the domain of <u>language and cognitive skills</u> has increased from 77% to 84%; in relation to <u>communication skills and general knowledge</u>, the increase is from 75% to 77%; for <u>emotional maturity</u>, the increase has been from 76% to 77%; for <u>social competence</u>, from 75% to 76%; and for <u>physical health and well-being</u>, a small increase from 77.7% in 2009 to 78.1% in 2018.

The other side of these figures is equally encouraging in most domains. The percentage of children "developmentally vulnerable" on one or more domain(s) has decreased, from 24% in 2009 to 22% in 2018, and on two or more domains, from 12% to 11% over the same period. These trends are apparent in most of the five domains: between 2009 and 2018, the percentage of vulnerable children in the domain of <u>language and cognitive skills</u> decreased from 9% to 7%; for <u>communication skills and general knowledge</u>, from 9% to 8%; and for <u>emotional maturity</u>, from 9% to 8%. For the domains of <u>social competence</u> and <u>physical health and well-being</u>, there was a small change in the other direction, with increases from 9.5% to 9.8%, and 9.3% to 9.6% respectively. Children classified as most vulnerable are more likely to perform poorly in primary school testing.

The attributes such as self-control, social skills, respectful behaviour, curiosity about the world, and literacy, numeracy, memory and communication skills measured by the AEDC are significant enablers for learning well in the early years of school, and underpin later academic performance.

When reported at a community level, the AEDC data show a gap between advantaged and disadvantaged areas that in 2018 is beginning to narrow in some domains. On the whole, children living in socio-economically disadvantaged locations are twice as likely to be vulnerable on one or more domains and nearly three times more likely to be vulnerable on two or more domains when compared with children from the least disadvantaged areas. Boys too are twice as likely as girls to be developmentally vulnerable on one or more and two or more domains. The domain where the difference between boys and girls is greatest is emotional maturity, where boys are more than three times as likely to be developmentally vulnerable as girls.

Children from households with a language background other than English (LBOTE) are more likely to be developmentally vulnerable than children in households which spoke only English, although there is almost no difference for children from an LBOTE household who are proficient in English.

This is the 'clean slate' on which schools then make their mark, ideally building on the strengths that the majority of children bring with them when they start school, and providing the necessary supports for the 20% of children who find it more difficult to adjust to being in a classroom and to learning.

Australian data - NAPLAN

NAPLAN testing of the fundamental skills of literacy and numeracy of Year 3, 5, 7 and 9 students is conducted annually, although no testing was carried out in 2020 when schools in some states were closed for various periods because of COVID-19. The NAPLAN program is managed by the Australian Curriculum, Assessment and Reporting Authority (ACARA), a joint Commonwealth and state-owned body established in 2008. At the time of writing, the results from the 2021 tests had just been reported. The 2021 results are compared with 2019 results, with previous years, and with the base year, which for numeracy, reading and conventions of language (spelling, grammar and punctuation) was 2008, and for writing was 2011.

For each year level and for each of the testing domains, NAPLAN results are reported publicly for Australia as a whole and for each jurisdiction in terms of the distribution of scores, average scores, and the proportion of students in each of ten achievement bands, including whether they are above, at or below the national minimum standard. Band 2 is the minimum standard for Year 3, Band 4 for Year 5, Band 5 for Year 7, and Band 6 for Year 9. High achievement is Band 6 and above for Year 3, Band 8 and above for Year 5, Band 9 and above for Year 7, and Band 10 for Year 9. A feature of the public discourse about NAPLAN has been the argument that this standard accepts a very slow rate of student progress and is set too low, well below international standards. For example, a student in Year 9 is considered to be meeting the minimum standard even if their reading skills are below a typical Year 5 student. ACARA is working at developing a new proficiency standard that will be harder to reach than the minimum standard. The introduction of the new standard may be a couple of years off yet.

When NAPLAN results are reported, comparisons are made between jurisdictions, between the performance of boys and girls, Indigenous and non-Indigenous students, students with a language background other than English and students from an English-speaking background, and between different locations – city, regional, and remote. Associations are also made with parental education and occupation.

The release of NAPLAN results each year is usually accompanied by a cacophony of voices criticising the tests and attempting to undermine their validity. Some of these criticisms have their foundation in ideological opposition to the tests at their introduction in 2008, a level of hostility that has not wavered over time, and appears to be accentuated when results are less than impressive. In recent years, criticisms have been levelled particularly at the administration of the tests, which have been making a transition to an online rather than paper-based platform, a process not without its technical and logistical problems. Disruption to the first on-line testing in 2019 in some schools because of connectivity issues was acknowledged when the results were reported, although in response to calls for the tests to be abandoned on the grounds of their unreliability, the assurance was given that the online and paper assessments had equal credibility and were measurable on the same scale. 2021 was a further transitional year to online testing, with the majority of students taking the tests online.

> *The release of NAPLAN results each year is usually accompanied by a cacophony of voices criticising the tests and attempting to undermine their validity.*

The 2021 results were reported in mid-December 2021, which meant that criticisms of the tests themselves were muted, overshadowed by other end-of-year preoccupations and by concerns about the impact on student performance of the many disruptions to schooling caused by the COVID-19 pandemic. Despite public expectations, the results showed no evidence that school lockdowns and home schooling had had a detrimental effect on student performance, either nationally or at the state level.

The official reporting on the overall results for 2021 emphasised a largely stable level of performance compared with 2019. In 2019, commentary had highlighted the fact that for students at most levels of schooling in most testing domains, the results were stagnant, or going backwards, defying the expectation that each subsequent cycle of testing will build on weaknesses identified in previous cycles, and therefore show improvement, at least by reducing the proportion of low achievers and raising the share of high achievers. An important purpose of basic skills testing such as NAPLAN is indeed to reveal areas of schooling requiring attention and to inform decisions on education policy, practices and resourcing. A failure to improve suggests that this objective of the tests is not being met.

Generally, the 2019 and 2021 NAPLAN results show trends similar to the international testing regimes. In most testing domains, and for secondary students in particular, results have not changed significantly from 2018, nor have they improved against the base years of 2011 for writing and 2008 for all other domains. Some improvement in average performance was measured in some domains for primary schools students, but for secondary students, average performance has either remained static or worsened.

To examine just the two domains of numeracy and writing, in 2021, in Years 3 and 5, the proportion of students achieving at or above the national minimum standard either improved marginally or remained static. In numeracy, 5% of Year 3 and Year 5 students failed to meet the minimum standard. In writing, the percentages were 3% for Year 3 students and 7% of Year 5 students. Achievement gaps widen however as students move through school. The results of particular concern are at the secondary level, with 5% of Year 7 students and 4% of Year 9 students failing to meet the national minimum standard in numeracy, and 9% of Year 7 students and 16% of Year 9 students failing to meet the standards in writing.

At the other end of the achievement spectrum, in most domains only a small proportion of students are achieving at a high level

– 17% of Year 3 students, 13% of Year 7 students and 7% of Year 9 students in numeracy and 18% of Year 3 students, 5% of Year 7 students and less than 4% of Year 9 students in writing. These results are consistent with Australia's relatively low proportion of high achievers in the PISA and TIMSS tests for secondary school students compared with the highest ranked countries. They compare for instance with the PISA maths and reading results of students in Singapore, the highest performing country, where 37% and 26% of students were high achievers.

There is a significant gap in the reading scores between boys and girls, a gap that is accentuated by the time students reach Year 9. In Year 3, 3% of boys and 2% of girls are at or below the national minimum standard. By Year 9, boys are twice as likely as girls to be at or below the standard. By Year 9, 11% of boys fail to achieve that benchmark, compared with 6% of girls. In numeracy, boys tend to outperform girls, but the gap is much narrower.

Students of parents with low education qualifications themselves have the lowest NAPLAN results, and conversely results are higher in all domains and at all year levels for students whose parents have higher levels of education and higher level occupations. As they progress through school, the children of parents with low education fall increasingly further behind, with a gap of ten months in Year 3 extending to 30 months by Year 9.

NAPLAN performance varies among states and territories, and between metropolitan and regional, rural and remote areas. The patterns of variability are fairly consistent from year to year, at all levels and in all domains. In the 2019 and 2021 tests, the average scores of students in the ACT, New South Wales and Victoria were generally above the national average while the other states tended to have scores below the national average. Results from the Northern Territory tend to be lower on average than the other states and territories. In relation to location, for Australia overall students attending schools in major cities have the highest average scores, while scores are lower in regional and remote areas, and lowest in very remote locations. While this is a consistent national pattern, in some jurisdictions there is little difference in the performance of students in locations outside a metropolitan area.

The argument is sometimes put that since NAPLAN results have not improved appreciably since the tests were introduced, the tests themselves should be abandoned. Given that the purpose of the tests is to produce objective data which can be used to identify problems in literacy and numeracy teaching and learning, a more responsible approach would be to use the data to investigate further those features of schools and approaches to schooling that influence performance. Objective and comparable performance information is critical evidence in the quest for improved school outcomes across the board and for particular groups of students.

In a word . . . some conclusions

A report card on the performance of Australian students might say, based on the evidence, that they are on average doing well, compared with the rest of the world, but they could do better, and they probably need to do better if the nation is to prosper economically and if today's students are to thrive in their adult lives. There is ample evidence about the characteristics of schools that are associated with better performance and a happier schooling experience. Not all of these can be addressed at the school level, but many of them can be, whatever the location of the school and the characteristics of the student body, with committed school leadership and the support of a knowledgeable and engaged school community.

Recognising what the real issues are and what can make a difference is important also in opening the door to improving the quality of Australian schooling through education policies and through targeting resources effectively. While this might ultimately manifest itself in better performance in national and international testing results, this is not the main game. Achieving the many recognised benefits to individuals and the nation of a high quality education system is the goal.

While there may be provisos to most research findings and numerous exceptions that prove the rule, there are many

> *A report card on the performance of Australian students might say, based on the evidence, that they are on average doing well, compared with the rest of the world, but they could do better, and they probably need to do better if the nation is to prosper economically and if today's students are to thrive in their adult lives.*

universally acknowledged truths about school quality that are well supported by data, research and experience.

A good starting point is the evidence that shows the impact quality schooling has on an individual's life after school – on one's personal, social and working life. It may be possible for a few people to have a healthy and productive life after a poor schooling experience, but for most of us, a quality education will greatly enhance our post-school possibilities. The evidence shows that the connection between quality schooling and the various elements of a good life is a causal one, and is even more important for students from a socio-economically disadvantaged background. Conversely, in the challenging environment of the present, with rapid social, economic and technological change, poor schooling outcomes will be even more devastating.

The connection is not direct because of a host of intervening factors, including the infinite variability of individuals and their circumstances, but to understand and appreciate the value of the school years and their potential influence is to take the first step as parents, grandparents and the Australian public in supporting those elements of schooling that matter most. It is also helpful to know that families who recognise the value of education and support their children's school help boost achievement.

The evidence highlights those features of schooling that are most important in achieving good outcomes for all students. The key factors come down to the quality of teachers and their teaching practices, having a high standard, coherent curriculum and consistent assessment, and a school climate that is orderly, that sets high expectations for student achievement and behaviour and that provides encouragement and support for such qualities as motivation, effort and persistence which underpin academic success but which also influence young people's life chances.

While some of these characteristics of quality schooling, such as the qualifications and attributes of the teaching workforce are subject to public policy decisions and the level of investment in schooling, many are within the control of individual schools and do not require ever-increasing levels of resources. A school community working together can make a difference to education outcomes for all the students in the school if they pay attention to those elements of schooling that are crucial for education success. And a public that is well informed about the critical aspects of education can influence governments to direct resources where they will make the most difference.

References

Australian Curriculum, Assessment and Reporting Authority (ACARA), 2019, *NAPLAN Achievement in Reading, Writing, Language Conventions and Numeracy: National report for 2019*, Sydney: ACARA

Carnine, D., 2000, *Why Education Experts Resist Effective Practices (And What It Would Take To Make Education More Like Medicine)*, Washington: Thomas P Fordham Foundation

Crato, Nuno, (ed), 2021, *Improving a Country's Education PISA 2018 Results in Ten Countries,* Springer, https://link.springer.com/book/10.1007%2F978-3-030-59031-4

Hanushek, E. A., Ruhose, J., and Woessmann, L., 2017, "Knowledge Capital and Average Income Differences: Development Accounting for US States," *American Economic Journal: Macroeconomics,* 9(4): 184-224

Hanushek, E. A. and Woessmann, L. 2019, Measurement counts: International student tests and economic growth, https://international-education.blog/en/2019/10/01/measurement-counts-international-student-tests-and-economic-growth/

Hanushek, E. A. and Woessmann, L. 2020, "A quantitative look at the economic impast of the European Union's educational goals," *Education Economics*, 28(3), 225-244

Hattie, J., 2009, *Visible Learning: A Synthesis of Over 800 Meta-Analyses Relating to Achievement,* London: Routledge

OECD Programme for International Student assessment (PISA), 2010, *The High Cost of Low Educational Performance:*

The Long-run Impact of Improving PISA Outcomes, Paris: OECD, https://www.oecd.org/pisa/44417824.pdf

OECD, 2020, *PISA 2018 Results (Volume I): What Students Know and Can Do*, PISA, OECD Publishing, Paris, https://doi.org/10.1787/5f07c754-en

OECD, 2020, *PISA 2018 Results (Volume II): Where All Students Can Succeed*, PISA, OECD Publishing, Paris, https://doi.org/10.1787/b5fd1b8f-en

OECD, 2020, *PISA 2018 Results (Volume III): What School Life Means for Students' Lives*, PISA, OECD Publishing, Paris, https://doi.org/10.1787/acd78851-en

OECD, 2020, *PISA 2018 Results (Volume V): Effective Policies, Successful Schools*, PISA, OECD Publishing, Paris, https://doi.org/10.1787/ca768d40-en

Thomson, S., Hillman, K., Schmid, M., Rodrigues, S., and Fullarton, J., 2017, *Reporting Australia's Results PIRLS 2016*, Melbourne: Australian Council for Educational Research (ACER)

Thomson, S., De Bortoli, L., Underwood, C., and Schmid, M., 2019, *PISA 2018: Reporting Australia's Results. Volume I Student Performance,* Melbourne: Australian Council for Educational Research (ACER)

Thomson, S., Wernert, N., Rodrigues, S., and O'Grady, E., 2020, *TIMSS 2019 Australia, Volume I Student Performance,* Melbourne: Australian Council for Educational Research (ACER)

www.ingramcontent.com/pod-product-compliance
Lightning Source LLC
Chambersburg PA
CBHW070400240426
43671CB00013BA/2579